TOP TRADITIONAL ROD AND CUSTOM BUILDERS

hot rod kings

DAVID PERRY • KEVIN THOMSON

FOREWORD BY **BILLY F GIBBONS**

For August—Follow your bliss.

For Patricia—Thank you for all your love and support.

First published in 2007 by Motorbooks, an imprint of MBI Publishing Company, Galtier Plaza, Suite 200, 380 Jackson Street, St. Paul, MN 55101 USA

MBI Publishing Company titles are also available at discounts in bulk quantity for industrial or sales-promotional use. For details write to Special Sales Manager at MBI Publishing Company, Galtier Plaza, Suite 200, 380 Jackson Street, St. Paul, MN 55101 USA

ISBN-13: 978-0-7603-2738-8
ISBN-10: 0-7603-2738-6

Library of Congress Cataloging-in-Publication Data

Thomson, Kevin, 1964-
   Hot rod kings : top traditional rod and custom builders / photography by David Perry; text by Kevin Thomson.
       p. cm.
   Includes index.
   ISBN-13: 978-0-7603-2738-8 (hardbound)
   ISBN-10: 0-7603-2738-6 (hardbound)
   1. Hot rods—Pictorial works. 2. Automobile engineers—United States—Biography. I. Perry, David, 1959- II. Title.
TL236.3.T535 2007
629.228'6092'273—dc22
                               2006024940

Editor: Dennis Pernu
Designer: Suzi Hutsell

Printed in Hong Kong

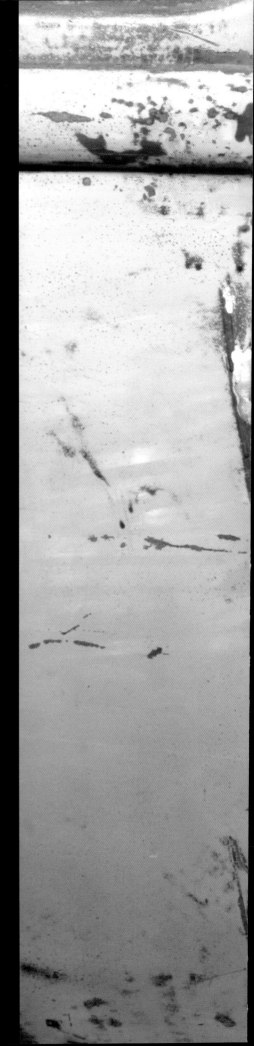

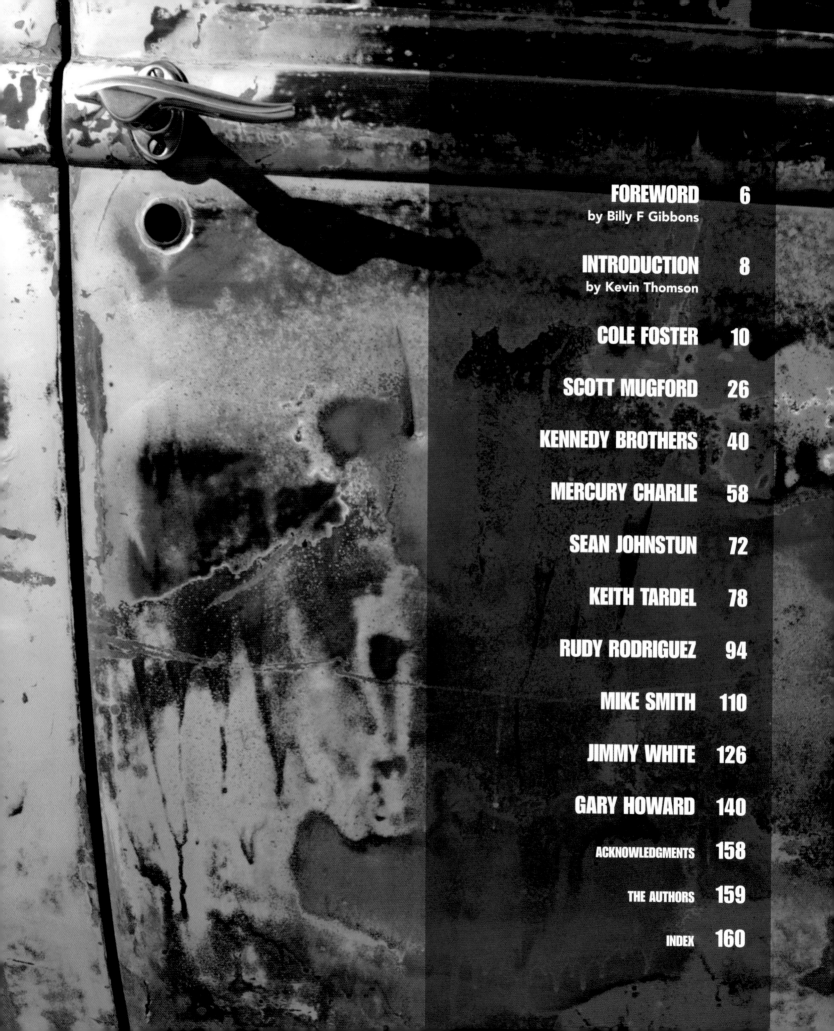

FOREWORD 6
by Billy F Gibbons

INTRODUCTION 8
by Kevin Thomson

COLE FOSTER 10

SCOTT MUGFORD 26

KENNEDY BROTHERS 40

MERCURY CHARLIE 58

SEAN JOHNSTUN 72

KEITH TARDEL 78

RUDY RODRIGUEZ 94

MIKE SMITH 110

JIMMY WHITE 126

GARY HOWARD 140

ACKNOWLEDGMENTS 158

THE AUTHORS 159

INDEX 160

BFG with his Rudy Rodriguez–built '32 highboy.

foreword

Hot Rod Kings...an intriguing title that begs the question, "Who are these guys?"

Well, here they are, thanks to the remarkable photographs of master lensman David Perry and the jumpin' prose of Kevin Thomson. A work showcasing the highlights of garage and backyard genius. Torch and stinger, hammer and block, steel and chrome. Tough stuff for sure.

As the pages here unfold, each one loaded with yet another hardcore look at true hot rodding as you like it, it's a challenge not to race on to the next 'coz this is the real deal. This ain't any retouched, refurbed dream scheme...it ain't Bondo, smoke, and mirrors...it's a gang of guys dedicated to their work and carrying on in a contemporary time frame, steadfastly keeping the hot rod tradition rockin' and rollin'.

Cole Foster, Gary Howard, Sean Johnstun, The Kennedy Brothers, Mercury Charlie, Scott Mugford, Rudy Rodriguez, Mike Smith, Keith Tardel, and Jimmy White are all wailin' away with their specialized methods of automotive madness. It's not necessarily how did they do this, but why. The answer? 'Coz they can. Fine, fine, fine!

Check out each frame. It tells a tale of what's up behind those secretive walls as the sparks fly and the panels are beaten. Loud and lean mean machines. Even though the craftsmen featured here are miles and miles apart, Perry and Thomson have captured their individual styles—styles of times that have gone by and reemerged into today. Fine, indeed.

Crank it up and enjoy.

—*Billy F Gibbons*

introduction

At the heart of this book is a story about mutual respect. The ten builders and one trimmer featured all know of each other and several are close friends. When the name of one is mentioned to another, the response is one of admiration or at the very least respect. This fact bears mention because a good reputation is hard to earn, much less keep, in a community as small as the one inhabited by the professional hot rod or custom builder.

So, these builders are in this book because their fellow hot rodders mentioned their names every time we asked them who their favorites were. In essence, they were chosen by their peers. The basic criteria were that each builder be a working professional, open to the public, and passionate about the craft he practices. Taking it a step further, David and I agreed that we wanted timeless design and no flavor-of-the-month B.S.

In keeping with the simple and well-thought-out elegance of the cars these people build, we decided to strip things down on our end as well. David forsook the standard "magic light" beauty shots for a straight-ahead glimpse into a day in the life of our subjects. On my end, I eschewed the traditional interview and chose a fly-on-the-wall approach. I observed and took notes on everything I saw, all the while with my tape recorder at the ready should conversation or relative commentary fill the air.

Typically, we'd arrive at a shop in the late morning, introduce ourselves, and then separate, David with his camera and me with my notebook. We wanted to stay as much out of the way as possible to allow whatever activities were taking place to happen at their natural pace. When it was time for lunch (almost always tacos), the tape recorder would come out and the lunchtime banter would be recorded. The rest of the afternoon would be spent hanging around the shop, driving around in a hot rod, or visiting a friend with a car built by the shop we were covering.

The days we spent visiting these shops were work, but only in the funnest sense of that word. The time that went into this book will remain in my mind as some of the finest I've ever spent and maybe the best job I've ever had. It has been a real privilege to get know these guys and I don't think I'll ever be able to thank them enough. They truly are Kings in every sense of the word.

—Kevin Thomson

Cole Foster

Salinas Boys

ABOUT A HUNDRED MILES SEPARATE SAN FRANCISCO FROM THE AGRICULTURAL TOWN OF SALINAS CALIFORNIA.

The trip takes just under two hours by car. If all the cars produced since 1950 were pulled off the streets of Salinas and some signage was knocked down, you'd be in a place not so different from the one in which Steinbeck lived. Under the modern veneer, it seems that not much has changed. Mountains still rise on all sides and long, flat fields of lettuce still surround the small western downtown. On the outskirts of town, some of the finest customs in the land have been rolling low and slow out of Cole Foster's "Salinas Boys" shop.

Cole's father was Pat Foster, driver and now restorer of dragsters and Funny Cars. In Cole's boyhood race car land of the San Fernando Valley, the sun shone strong, and bicycle, skateboard, and car culture were everywhere. Going to the track to watch Dad race and to help with the cars was part of Cole's day-to-day existence. The simple solutions and quality inherent in the construction of the dragsters had a profound influence on Cole. Despite the initial yearnings to be a racer, too, Cole also wanted to be a fine artist. "I wanted to paint and draw," he recalls. "I liked sculpture as far as ceramics. Artist guys like Kenny Youngblood would send me Xeroxes of that year's Funny Car and dragster body styles and I'd color 'em in." In the days before the cars came along, Cole says, "We were the guys with the bitchin' bicycles and building models, and were doin' stuff way before we got into cars." Yes, always messing around.

Cole finished his sophomore year in the San Fernando Valley only to be uprooted and relocated to the Carmel Valley by his newly remarried dad. It was a big change in scenery, culture, and demographics, and race cars were no longer a part of his or his dad's life. Cole kept messing around with cars, only now it was sports cars. The BMW 2002 he drove became a test bed for early custom antics like shaved door handles and lowering. One of his dad's neighbors, Dave Smith, had a paint shop that he let Cole

Kirk Hammett's 1936 Ford three-window coupe. This car started out as a five-window that Cole and crew fearlessly turned into a chopped three-window. Check out the subtly and beautifully modified windshield shape. A modern fuelie Ford small-block provides the power. Not seen in this photo are the hood sides or the custom hubcaps Cole created just for this car.

and his friends use after hours. Cole also got some fabrication chops by hanging around the shop of the local Gravelle brothers, whose family ran stock cars.

On the streets of Salinas, the hot rod coupes of George and Buck Thomas were king, and Cole and his friend, Job Stevens, were duly impressed. The Thomases had built their cars, and they started passing on their knowledge to Cole and Job. Cole went out and got a '55 Chevy, and Job a '54. It wasn't long before the urge to chop came along. Job's went first, with the sage advice of Butch Hurley. Cole and Job also started mixing flattener into the paint to give their cars a suede look. They began going to Paso Robles and that's when the custom hook really took for Cole.

In 1988, Cole bought the '54 Chevy hardtop he still has to this day and refers to as "the Blue Car." Cole chopped it and set the roof back down with Job, Don Fretwell, and Buck Thomas. The proportions were dead nuts and Cole's reputation began to grow. To get out of the restaurant business, Cole and his friends started to work cars on the side. They did paint jobs, collision work, and mechanical stuff. By the early 1990s, the hobby had become the life.

Before late 2006, when Cole and his wife, Susan, acquired their current 1940s Spanish Revival home with complete shop facilities out back, Cole and the Salinas Boys built the cars and bikes that earned their cred in a space that he had moved into in 1990. It's the same space you see on these pages. Nothing special, no sign, just a standard industrial-grade steel building on the outskirts of town. The living quarters were directly above the workspace and had a low,

Thomas Torjeson, Cole Foster, and Jordan Skow.

16

Cole muggin' in the hand-hammered aluminum Stetson he made hisself.

steel roof for a ceiling. This was dedication and economic necessity. Ask anyone who's ever sacrificed "normal" living for their passion and they'll tell you it isn't always easy; in the same breath they might tell you they wouldn't trade it for the world. Eventually, it becomes the norm, and the McMansion on the hill with the big screen, four-car, and yardman takes on an alien vibe.

Cole's 1990–2006 shop consisted of two garages. One was given over to store completed projects, up-and-comers, and "the Blue Car." The side that Cole and Susan lived over was the clean, working side. Like any good shop, it had its fair share of art and pop/car culture to keep your mind clicking. As you walked through the front door, a tiny, well-equipped machine shop sat to your right. A half-finished bike was in your way, and on the wall to your left was the library— all 20 feet of it. Any and all aspects of car and motorcycle culture, construction, and style are represented in Cole's collection. Inspiration, information, what to do, and what not to do are right at Cole's fingertips. "It's nice to be able to sit down with some books," Cole explains.

A well-stocked and well-thumbed library says a lot about its owner. It represents a certain amount of care, passion, and hunger—three essential ingredients Cole puts into the cars he and his crew build. Care is in the well-thought-out construction underneath the coachbuilder fit and finish. Passion is in the incredible hand-hammered and finished metal work. Hunger is in the design ideas that transcend those of the by-the-book, cookie-cutter customizer. Hunger also represents the desire to improve and change, to evolve.

Underneath a collection of neon from Salinas' past sat the very latest in the evolution of Cole and the Salinas Boys' aesthetic and technique. Appropriately, a poster of Hendrix astride a chopper gazed down on the project, the commission of Kirk Hammett, lead guitarist of Metallica. Kirk wanted a three-window coupe in the custom, not hot rod, vein. A '36 Ford would do fine. Cole agreed but could not find one suitable for the job. A clean five-window came up and Cole took it.

These shots give some idea of the cramped but complete machine tool room at the old shop.
To the left of Marilyn is the "Harvester of Bondo."

A five-window into a three-window? Yes, and with tons of work. A trunk lid built from scratch, front fenders blended into the running board, a homemade grille blended into the front fenders, top chopped, window removed and blended. Cole reworked the front- and rear-window openings and sectioned the tops of the doors to preserve side-glass proportioning. There's a handmade hood; in-house frame and chassis on air bags; custom taillights with shop-built stainless bezels; and leather interior. Taking inspiration from Westergard and European coachbuilders, Cole and his boys, Thomas Torjeson, Jordan Skow, and painter Jesse Cruz, have created a work of art. It is comparable to the one-off, round-door Art Deco 1934 Rolls-Royce created by the Belgian coachworks of Henri Jonckheere way back in the day. Where the Rolls is sleek, yet massive, Cole's '36 is svelte and slippery.

Rolling down the street, from any angle, the three-window looks like a sculpted piece of obsidian. The lines flow from the front, then tighten at the rear like haute couture eveningwear. There is elegance and evil lurking here. This car is a Prohibition-era whiskey baron's town ride. But instead of bourbon, the trunk is loaded with an electric guitar and amplifier, all custom-fitted, of course.

Proportionately, the car is perfect and has become the new iconic coupe. "I never took metal shop and I knew I wasn't going to go to college, so this is pretty much fine art to me," says Cole. "There's not much art out there I don't think I could not do. I don't think I'm the greatest painter in the world; I saw pretty early that I had to work at it technically. There are some people that just have it and it's so magical.... I have a good mind's eye to see what I want to do. It takes years to be able to do that physically on a car, to learn the skill. I could just as easily direct, but I had to do it myself."

Cole does not screw around with his work. He is constantly working with his head and his hands. The eyes are always looking to separate the wheat from the chaff. He builds with those eyes turned toward timeless by taking cues from all aspects of design, from locomotives to airplanes, from furniture to automobiles. The Salinas Boys shop is focused on classic design that won't look tired when the trend is spent and wadded up in reruns of how-to, bolt-on shows at three in the morning.

Cole's now-famous chopped '54 Chevy "blue car" rests in the storage area, with a '32 five-window behind it.

When it comes to contemporary trends and designs, Cole gets heated and the words fly. He spits, "I'm pretty passionate about [designing and building]. Is the talent pool so small that they let some fucking guy from Blink 182 design wheels? I feel like I could do any of that shit. I've knocked on the door and I don't get a shot. Other guys in my world that are supposed to be customizers, that have never changed a tire, get 10 of them. I went to SEMA and saw wheels with actual diamonds in them, spinning around. I came back so fucked up by it that I wanted to quit.... It's hard to get through the bullshit. There are customizers out there that lip-synch. They don't build it. They don't touch it. They build theme bikes. I can't relate at all. Why don't these guys come over and do cars? What would they do? Make an Orca? 'This would be a nice killer whale '36.' It's so far off. If I did that, people would laugh, but with the bike thing they would applaud, like, 'That's a nice space shuttle. Nice job on the space shuttle bike.' It makes me wanna blow my head off. If that's mainstream, then I'm way out of it."

To be out of the mainstream in taste, aesthetics, career choice, and beliefs has always been the day-to-day reality for many artists. For people of Cole's generation, born in the 1960s, the influence of skateboarding, punk rock, and the DIY ethic of the American underground music and arts culture cannot be underestimated. Cole and his cohorts still skate and the shop conversation swings easily from fabricating custom motorcycle gas tanks to shredding gnarly coping in a backyard pool. Both activities are creative, and when done well, individualistic. It all relates directly to where Cole is now. The life of the dedicated customizer is no social whirlwind. It can be filled with single-minded activity executed alone or with one or two friends.

Now, as the '36 nears completion, Cole and the Boys have their sights set more and more on motorcycles. Cole has done several, and his "Blue Bobber" has come to be viewed as a truly new and individual statement. With all the fuss going on about choppers these days, Cole has built one that has risen above the rest of the billet, "space shuttle" bikes of the day. The tank on the Blue Bobber is Cole's own design

Some of Cole's bikes, including, left to right: a custom Harley, Beautiful Loser, and the famous "blue bobber."

and will soon be in full production at Custom Chrome. The lost wax-cast beehive oil tank is already being copied. Cole has also designed a line of classy and functional grips that look like they have been turned from chunks of swirly Bakelite.

Why this focus on bikes from a guy who made his mark with cars? Cole just points to the trunk lid of the '36 and explains, "I can do ten motorcycles or that trunk. That trunk has more time in it than every motorcycle I've done bodywork for. The cars are so labor-intensive and the bar is so high. It's pretty easy for me to go over and do bikes. It's not shooting fish in a barrel, but there's a lot of unexplored territory." Unexplored territory is where Cole and the Salinas Boys seem the most comfortable.

Everybody at the shop is skilled in his own way and they all bring a unique viewpoint. Thomas Torjeson has boat-crafting and metal-fabrication skills, which he combines with an endless bag of electromechanical tricks. Jordan Skow hooked up with Cole in 2005 when he paid Cole 20 bucks to crash on a hotel floor at Paso Robles. Jordan is a luthier by trade and brings knowledge of woodcrafting, inlay techniques, and wiring to the shop. "Old-timer" Jesse Cruz does the finish work and lays down the smoothest paint. Cole's old friend, Job Stevens, is still around, but mainly doing his own thing at his place across the way.

Cole is definitely the main man, but he is no straw boss. The atmosphere at the shop is more collaborative than fascist. Cole says, "I'm not a Nazi. It's not 'my way or that's it.' I like people I respect around me to give me their input. I like to take that input and people can change my mind. If we all came from the same background, it would be kinda boring in a way...you wouldn't have as much stuff to kick around. I like to kick around ideas and if you do that, you get to a level where you can bring it up two notches." Like in music, or any other art form, Cole and the crew know that strength is in collaboration. Cole may be the lead visionary, but his trust in those around him helps him to focus and hone his vision into the cars and bikes the shop puts out.

The quality of a Salinas Boys custom speaks for itself, yet nobody is getting rich over here. The work is difficult and sometimes tedious. Custom fabrication requires a will to not only start something, but to start something and then throw it away—sometimes over and over. The hours are long and evident on Cole's face, and as he lights another cigarette, he lays it out. "Nobody's gonna come in here and do this car in a week," he says, nodding to Hammett's '36. "It takes so much labor. There is no quick way to do it. The cars are out of control. The bar is so high to do one that stands out at all.... It's hard to keep a customer pumped up for two years while the car is being built. A good housepainter probably makes more money. You can do that out of a van. I've got two shop spaces and all this machinery, and I still give away half my time. It's self-inflicted. But this is fun for us, the problem-solving. It's fun to take the air and say, 'I'm gonna make a bracket here,' or design something and do it. It's fun."

It's fun. Yet, heed the words above. In a sense they are saying, "Mommas, don't let your babies grow up to be hot rodders." Well, only if you don't want an inspirational, free thinker on your hands.

The stairway to the former living quarters above the former shop.

23

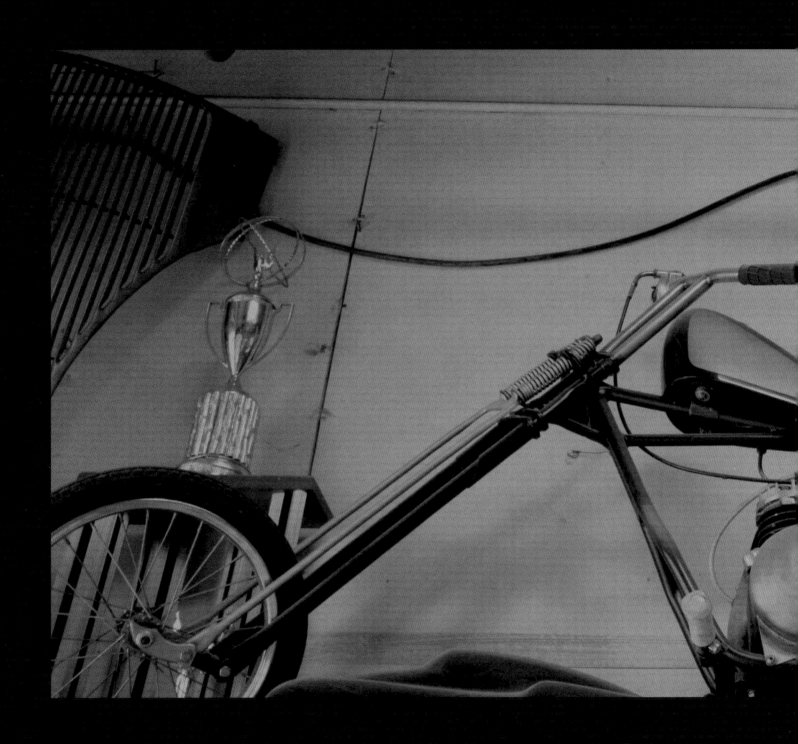

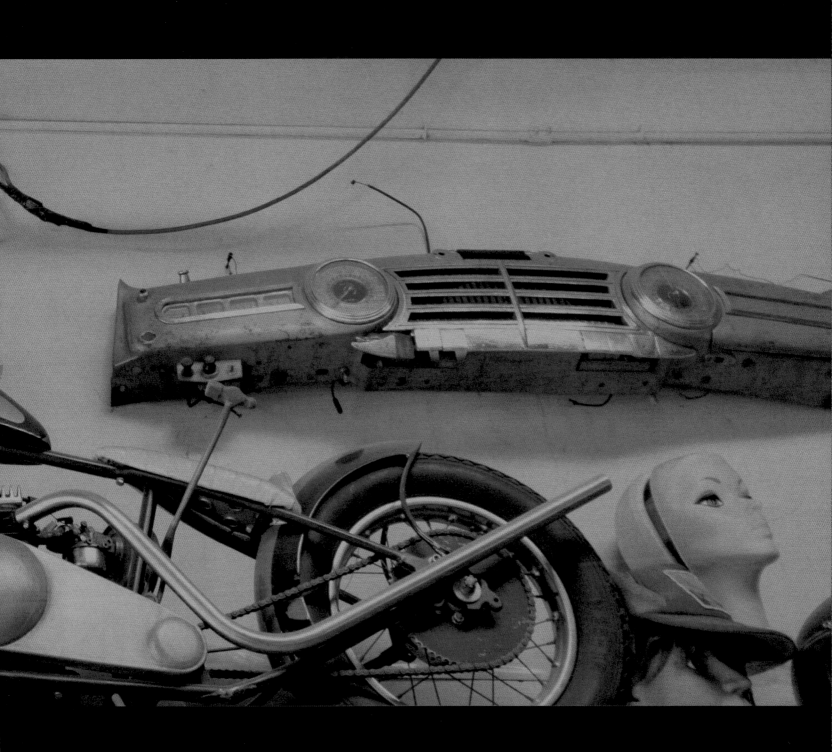

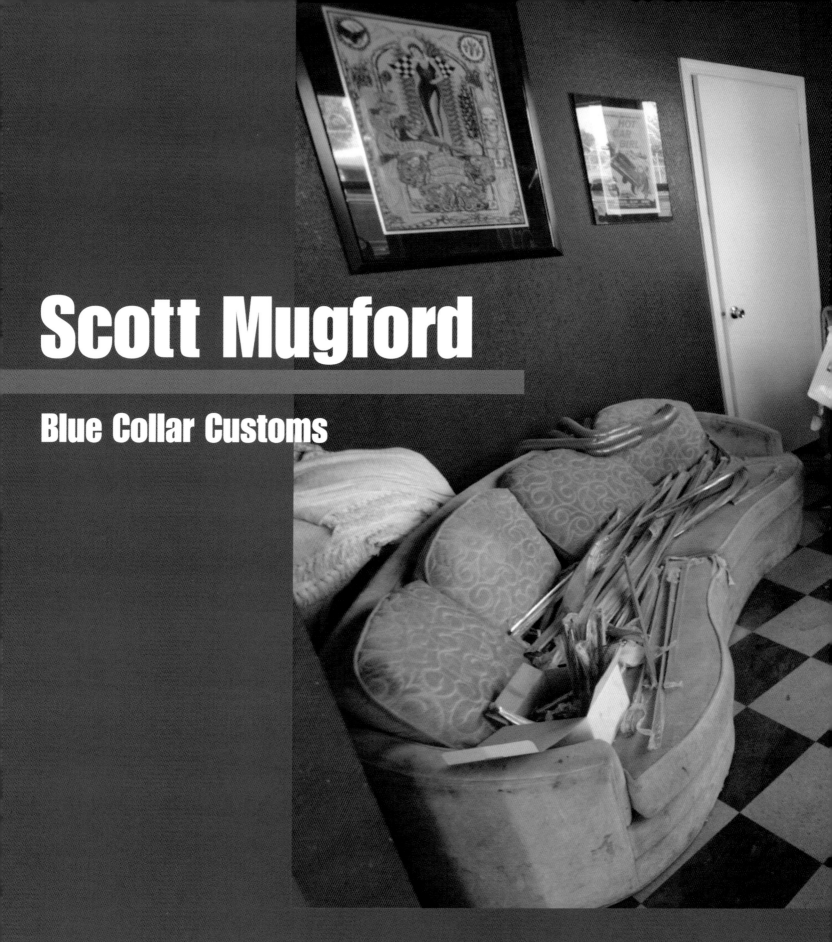

Scott Mugford

Blue Collar Customs

Scott Mugford, Rob Cannon, and Phil Cannon.

Strip clubs, strip malls, and a relic of Space Age roadside architecture called Orbits sitting on a corner, dispensing gasoline. The building looks more like a traditional Dutch woman's fieldworker hat than anything ever sent into orbit, but what the heck. The few people who are walking look nearly as worn as the buildings that surround them. You could be almost anywhere in California, but this is definitely NoCal; trees with leaves are in the majority here.

Turn one of many funky corners and here is what you see: The first building on the left is a tow yard with the usual bumper crop of '80s and '90s beaters that obscure something very interesting next door. The colors in the lot next door catch the eye. Faded grays, reds, yellows, charcoal blacks, and rust adorn beautifully shaped sheet metal.

The sentinel at the gate is a bone stock '53 Studebaker Hawk in a faded pale yellow suit. Keeping it company is an in-progress '52 Ford.

James Hetfield's 1936 Ford five-window coupe, chopped and bagged by Blue Collar Customs.

Phil Cannon

Check it out. Walk up to it and see the visible scar of a section job on the quarter panel disappear at the door and front fender that bear no scars, yet have the same proportion as the quarter panel. Very sneaky, very tricky, and subtle. The door and fender skin appear untouched in their original paint. It's the first sign of the metalworking prowess of the badasses at Blue Collar Customs. They're bad, not yet nationwide, and low-key. Nothing flashy, barely a sign to let you know where you're at, but once you're in the gate you know you are indeed where it is at.

Aside from the Stude and Ford "welcome wagon," the rest of the starting (or nonstarting) lineup lays down the hot rod and custom rule. Some of the cars are done, some are not, and others are awaiting a decision. The '55 Imperial is there to donate its 331-ci hemispherical iron lung to a roadster. There's a sweet '29 Ford roadster pickup for sale, and next to that is an uncut '29 Model A sedan. A '55 Nomad with a '58 Brookwood hangs out next to a Caddy convertible, and in the far corner linger the truly hard cases. These tough nuts are in pieces and filed under "someday": a '31 Dodge touring car, a near-dead roadster body and floor with two seats and a firewall. Looking at these shot-down cars and giving them a whole new life in your imagination is part of the fun. Plotting the stages of construction, transformation, and finish details make up the rest of the mind game. But taking the tools to the steel ain't no mind game, hoss, and inside the Blue Collar Customs shop is where it all explodes, then reanimates.

The shop's front room isn't much in the way of creature comfort, but it does have a couple of cool pieces on the walls, so check 'em, give the tiki some love, and keep walking. The control center is bare bones and contains the four necessities: a fridge, a chair, a computer, and a phone. Two more steps and you're out in the shop where it's all business and very busy. Not immaculate, not even neat, the shop looks like an around-the-clock affair. A massive arc welder, a sheetmetal break, an English wheel, a hundred hammers, and a press belie the heavy metal rework going on here.

It's only a four-bay shop a little over 3,500 square feet and there is just enough room to work the rods and toss in a chopper or two. Like any group of dedicated pack rats, there are cool bits and pieces everywhere. If you look up into the attic, it gets even heavier. There's a funky homemade roadster up there built from plans set out in *Car Craft* in the early '70s. There are also wheels, hoods, cowls, lamp assemblies, steering wheels, dust, and rust. Everything you might need to help you cross the finish line on a project that stalled.

In bay number one, there is a stranger in the house of steel. It's a '64 Impala in the grand lowrider style of the '80s. *Everything*

Drew Trinidad's 410 Buick-powered '29 Model A sedan. This car is chopped 5 1/2 inches and channeled 5 inches. In the rear there's a Ford 9-inch hung on a triangulated four-bar suspension sprung with Toyota truck torsion bars.

A look inside Blue Collar Customs will be met by plenty of vintage tin, in this case a '58 Impala and '37 Ford (above), and a '38 Ford and '52 Chevy (below).

is engraved; *las Bonitas Loca* grace the underhood sheet metal. The windshield claims the car to be "King of the Boulevard," while the side glass spells it out "BOULIVARD." It's bad, and like it says on the back glass, "take notes." The proprietors, Scott Mugford, Phil Cannon, and Rob Cannon, took on the lowrider even though it's not really their scene. The owner of the '64 likes the work the boys do, and was persistent until they caved. There will be plenty of fab work, like a gullwing trunk, to keep the boys interested. And how the fuck do you say no to the King of the Boulivard anyway?

Further into the shop, a '50 Ford coupe is in mid-chop. Nearly a full 5 inches have come out already. The interior is braced all to hell and the surgery is plain to see. This is no amateur hour here, and all three of the guys get into it. Each one of them brings a particular set of skills to the table and they share those skills to the max, making the trio ever stronger.

Scott isn't afraid to chop a top and he's also responsible for that sneaky door and fender section job on the Ford out front. All the sectioning happened backstage, then the curtain was drawn, cut, and folded under at the bottom, leaving no trace. By Scott's own admission, it's the chassis work that really gets the blood runnin'. A good example of Scott's chassis fab is on Drew Trinidad's Model A sedan. The rear is suspended by a triangulated four-bar with the top bars flipped backward and sprung by latitudinal, cut-down Toyota truck torsion bars. Weird? Yes. Functional? Yes. Cool? Yes.

Rob Cannon is the quiet one with a lot on his mind. All the guys pitch in with ideas on style and design, but Scott says,

Rob Cannon

This meanie is a 1930 Model A being built for James Hetfield to NHRA-legal 9.90-second specs. The chassis is scratchbuilt at Blue Collar. The Buick drums hide a Wilwood disc system. Scott fabbed all the bracketry as well.

Phil and Rob are both into the bobber vibe. Up front is Phil's '01 Harley with custom frame and tank riding stop airbags. In back is Rob's '57 hardtail panhead.

"Rob's the one with the rad eye." It ain't about rulers and tape measures all the time; it's about the eye and the look, and Rob knows where "right" is. Rob's no slouch with the torch and grinder either, and he takes good care of a lot of the mechanical beeswax too. His skill with the paper trail left behind by these nuts and bolts is the key to solvency for "BCC."

Phil Cannon (no relation to Rob) brings a family tradition of customizing and chopping cars to the shop, along with his easygoing demeanor. His dad was chopping 'em back in the day and passed on the knowledge that Phil put to good use at his first shop, Crown Customs, and now at Blue Collar. He's probably chopped over 60 cars and there is no end in sight. He's mostly into '50s-style customs, but he won't shirk when it's time to chop that full-height Model A down to proper size.

Blue Collar Customs is low-profile, yet it puts the hammer to the steel full stop. They do completes as well as partials, like the sheet-metal work surrounding the Buick grille laid into the nose of Jim Luke's six-bangin' '52 Chevy coupe. Ya see, no job too small, brother, and the boys stay very much alive by doin' it all. There is a driving philosophy behind Blue Collar Customs and *driving* is what it's all about.

Case in point would be Craig Kovarik's '50 Lincoln. It used to be four-door and now it has only two. Blue Collar chopped it nearly 8 inches "'til it looked cool," and channeled using by the same criteria. It's ragged, but right, because there is no mud whatsoever on this car, and the lines from the drastic rework are there for interested parties to see and ponder. The cosmetic side of the equation is going to have to wait for the bank account to fatten up. For now, the world looks mighty fine through that chopped windshield and Craig has fun hitting the streets in a variety of ride heights courtesy of the BCC-installed airbag suspension.

On the "complete" side of the coin is Dean Anderson's '29 Model A roadster. This ride is all patina all the time, right down to the rims. The car barks "cool"

Scott Mugford

Scott's daughter Hannah practices for the day she can drive Dad's '28 Model A.

out the rude and crude side pipes that travel the passenger side and dump, chopper-style, above and just behind the rear tire. Makin' all that racket is a Mercedes-Benz six banger. Dual carbs, split manifold, and a faded and polished aluminum valve cover make it hot rod all the way, despite the German lineage. The mill looks and functions just right in front of the channeled Model A roadster body. There's plenty of detail too: a surfboard-shaped steel loud pedal, a visible driveline striped by Dean's lady, Stacy Cooper, a '40 Chevy truck dash, copper-pipe radiator plumbing, and an MG steering wheel all put in equal time to make this ride the bad one that it is. Dean and Stacy drive the wheels off this thing, and it made the trek from Sacto to Bonneville without a hitch for the 2005 Speed Week.

In 2006, Blue Collar got some higher-profile commissions from Metallica frontman James Hetfield. One is a punk rock version of Kirk Hammett's '36 Ford coupe by Cole Foster. Hetfield's '36 is a five-window that is mean and dirty where Hammett's is smooth and svelte. Blue Collar chopped it 5 inches and laid in a whole new suspension to replace the lame Camaro subframe and 5-inch lowering blocks. Scott C-notched the frame 8 inches, put in drop spindles, and set the car on airbags. Hetfield did some of the work himself and Scott claims he's just like one of the boys when it comes to getting dirty on a hot rod. The other car that Hetfield commissioned the boys to do is an all-out, ground-up 1930 Tudor slated for 9.90-second drag racing. The in-house frame features drilled-and-filled front horns, tubular crossmembers, and a scratch-built roll cage. A 427-ci Chevy stroker will provide the power. As of this writing, the car is still

James Hetfield's evil 1936 Ford five-window. A steel hood has since replaced the chains.

Above: Dean Anderson's '29 A roadster with its six-cylinder Mercedes-Benz power. The body is channeled over original Model A rails.

Left: Dean's roadster features an MG wheel, '40 Chevy truck dash, a grenade-shifted C4 auto trans, and a cool little surfboard gas pedal.

under construction but already looks like a take-no-prisoners effort from Scott and the Blue Collar crew.

Cool, oddball engine and trans combos are part of the fun at BCC, but Scott doesn't turn up his nose at the venerable 350/350 combo, either. "If it's what you can afford and it makes the difference between driving or not driving the car, then go for it," he says. "Change the motor later if you want." The same goes for paint or no paint, patina, or primer. The difference here is getting the cars on the road with real craftsmanship and on a workingman's budget. And, no, BCC doesn't do dial-a-part, bolt-together street rods. "We're never gonna be a street rod shop. I'd hang myself first," says Scott. It's all about the attitude and the parts used in the build. No crushed velour, DVD-playin' billet hoopdies here. Rat rod trend or not, these guys are in for the long haul and always have been. They are busy enough to be contemplating the move to a bigger shop and Scott is planning a four-cylinder, rear-engine modified roadster for Bonneville.

Once you are behind the wheel, enjoying the ride Blue Collar Customs created for you, the inspiration for finishing touches or major changes can hit anytime, anywhere. When they do and your ducks are all in a row, drive right back through the gate at BCC and tell the boys to have at it. They'll gladly oblige.

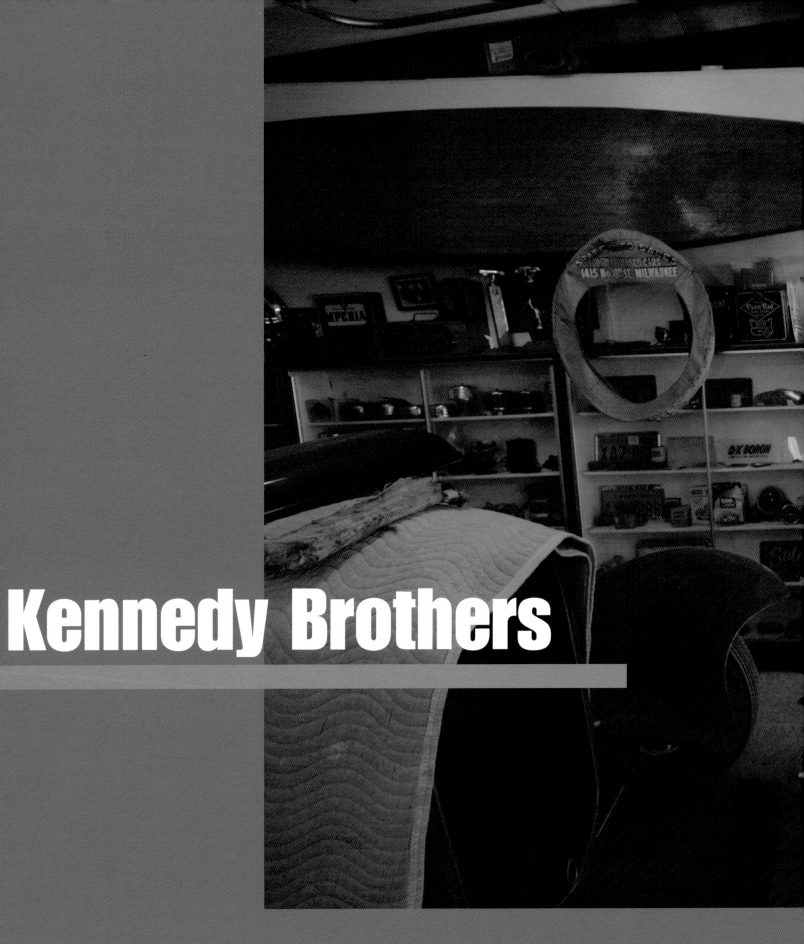

Kennedy Brothers

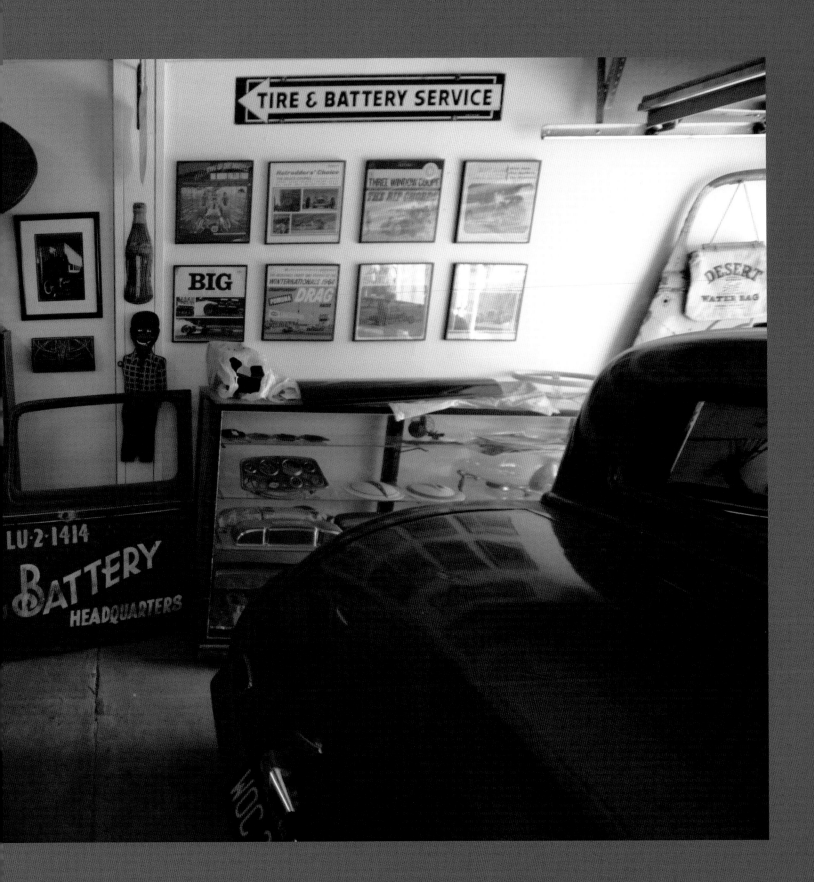

Jason Kennedy

Joe Kennedy

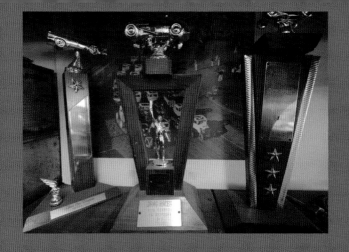

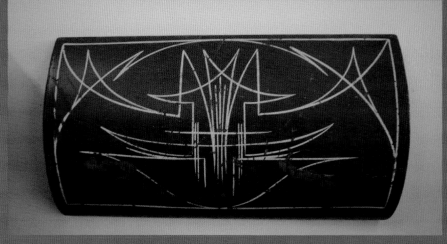

J
OE AND JASON KENNEDY WERE BORN FOUR YEARS APART AND GREW UP IN THE URBANIZED DESERT EAST OF LOS ANGELES.

Their father was a hot rodder who made his living repainting and restoring early painted automotive wood grain. Their mother ran an antique shop and the love of all things old was passed on to the boys. Swap meets, auctions, and estate sales were a big part of their childhood. That background serves the Kennedy Brothers well today.

Despite growing up inland in Whittier, the brothers were constantly on the coast catching waves or skating the parks when the ocean was flat. Being part of the surf/skate faction and not fitting in with the mainstream "in crowd" at high school meant the brothers hung out with the punks. "The punks were the only ones who would accept us, and we really didn't have many friends, surf-wise," Joe recalls about his teenage years. The aggressive music of the '80s punk scene is still in heavy rotation at the Kennedy Brothers' shop. CDs and cassettes by the Butthole Surfers, Youth Brigade, Fear, and the Go-Nuts rub elbows with Black Sabbath and The Damned.

The brothers are close, a bond perhaps reinforced by their outsider status as teens. They each in turn inherited their mom's '67 El Camino to drive to high school and pick up girls. Everyone in town associated the brothers with that car. As they got older, they began restoring bicycles and then went

Shop hounds Da Vinci (left) and Sinatra (right).

43

into a cottage business restoring auto spotlights like the Appletons seen on so many '50s customs. Meanwhile, anything that was cool and old began to accumulate.

Both Joe and Jason are friendly, soft-spoken, and direct. In conversation, Joe makes direct eye contact while keeping a secondary focus on whatever task may be at hand. Jason, on the other hand, keeps his focus on the task and then breaks for bursts of conversation. The Kennedys will give you their attention, but not at the expense of work to be done. It's a useful skill, as SO-CAL Speed Shop is just around the corner and folks frequently drop by the Kennedy shop, too.

A visit to the Kennedy Brothers' shop is worth whatever sidetrack you have to take to get there and whatever time you have to sacrifice. It's located on a piece of land in a residential/industrial section of Pomona. The city boomed in the 1950s and into the early '60s, then the plug was pulled and the town began to languish. Large

Victorian homes wreathed in decay sit side by side with habitable bungalows, both fronted by weed-choked sidewalks. Nothing, aside from middle-class flight, appears to have happened in 20 years.

Right-hand man Lance Soliday puttin' in the hours.

The Venice Beach survivor. A heavily channeled '32 three-window the Kennedy Brothers made roadworthy again.

On the main drag, an early McDonalds restaurant with arches piercing the glass and stainless structure still clings to life. Only nowadays, it's doughnuts instead of burgers scenting the nearby air. Old signage and a sawdust-floor sandwich shop next to the railroad complete the urban picture. When the wind blows out the smog, the mountains reappear and the scene takes on a Technicolor movie-lot atmosphere. It just feels old, and what better place for an automotive shop that deals in nothing newer than 1936?

Low, boxlike residences with old, tall trees and rusting heavy equipment for décor bound the shop property. There is no sign out front to let passersby know there is a hot rod shop at the address. The bare dirt driveway leads to a latticed chainlink gate that keeps curious street-side eyes from seeing in. For security and personal sanity, a pair of Italian greyhounds, Sinatra and Da Vinci, have the run of the place. Should strangers appear at the gate, the dogs sound the general alarm. Once you are OK'd by the masters, they quickly become your new best friends.

The goings-on behind the gates become obvious once they are opened. To the immediate left is a rust pile with some faded Cragars bolted to a Ford 9-inch. The El Camino is parked next to a boot-brown roadster that belongs to full-timer Lance Soliday. A friend's '40 Ford project and a Fordor complete the first 30 feet of your journey into Kennedy Land.

Woodies, longboards, minibikes. Whatever the Kennedys are into and have space for is on the premises.

This car was built by the Brothers in 60 days and then driven from the shop in Pomona, California, to the Lonestar Round Up in Austin, Texas. A '49 8BA flathead dressed out with Harrell heads and intake with two 97s on top powers this ultra-clean highboy Deuce roadster. A fully chromed suspension accentuates just how tight and shiny this car really is. In keeping with the Brothers' strictly traditional theme, a '32 trans telegraphs the power to a '32 rear.

The shop buildings are rectangular, bleached-white, one-story affairs set in an L configuration and bound by shipping containers, parts racks, and chainlink on the right. The sunny central courtyard has enough room to work on two or three cars. Vintage signage adorns the walls and hangs from the eaves. Out back, from the base of the L, is more storage, chock-a-block with wheels, wishbones, fenders, and frames.

The base of the L also serves as the indoor work area. Even though Lance is knee-deep in a '32 Ford Fordor project, the work area is neat as a pin. The walls have all manner of signage, drawings, snapshots, and adverts catching eyes from beneath a layer of carbon and dust. Tools abound, many of them nearly as old as the cars they are set upon to work. The gray and black blurs of Sinatra and Da Vinci race through the space, oblivious to the work that surrounds their play.

The long and low building that makes up the stem of the L is used for storage of cars, parts, and an incredible collection that includes everything from complete cars to anything the Kennedys deem cool. There are toy cars and models of cars. Skateboards from the clay-wheel era to the present are lined up. Parts abound, from barrels of axles to air cleaners, intake manifolds, carburetors, and any sort of accessory you can imagine. All of this shares the space with a tiki bar, records, jukeboxes, Spanish galleons, radios, bicycles, and a great collection of vintage long boards that Joe and Jason surf on every weekend. And, of course, there are the cars.

In the storage area alone there are five cars, two in running condition and the other three just napping. One of the runners is a '32 three-window, channeled more than 6 inches and chopped around 5 inches, with a faded copper paint job that sucks you right into its orbit. The car was found in Venice, California, and built sometime in the early '70s. It's all steel, with an old Offy 360 intake on top of a 302-ci Chevy. An early four-speed hydro slush box serves as a transmission, sending the power back to an Olds rear. The car rolls on five-spoke Americans with pie-cutters up front and cheater slicks in the rear. Everything about the car is somehow just right and the Kennedys know it. No big changes are planned for this one. They stopped at making the car safer and reworking the damaged grille shell. You could probably shake an eighth of Thai stick out of the brown shag carpet, but it's not coming out anytime soon and neither is the oddball Coors tap handle shifter that resides right between your legs.

The other runner is Jason's '32 Ford three-window. This car has one of the coolest patinas ever. A Hot Wheels–esque metallic lime green was the last color to be sprayed onto the steel years ago. It is now in full desert fade and gives way to black, primer, and bare steel. Ancient runs and drips that were sanded down years ago still show their outlines through the layers of paint. The Chevy small-block between the rails reflects the Kennedy aesthetic. Bead-blasted, raw-aluminum Corvette valve covers, cast-iron ram's horn exhaust, and a bare-aluminum single four intake keep the motor low-key and in play with the rest of the car.

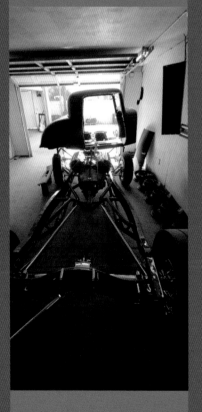

Jason Kennedy's perfectly patinaed '32 five-window sports a 283-ci Chevy V-8.

Sleeping in the back row are Joe's '32 Ford coupe, an untouched '32 Ford pickup, and a flathead-powered rail job. Joe would love to work on the '32 some more, but he's running a business and can only work whatever 80 hours a week he chooses. The rail job gets him pretty excited, but there are no plans to change it at all. Joe tells the story like this: "It was Bill Brodack's car, The Iron Horse. Bill got it in '69 and raced and bracket-raced it until '73. The car is still the same as Bill left it in '73, totally untouched. Several folks have claimed it started as an Ivo car, but we've never verified that. It's definitely a Fuller chassis. I love cars like this, found just the way they are."

The '32 Fordor that Lance Soliday is working on for customer Jim Jard shows off the Kennedys' build style as well as some departures. The genuine '32 frame is only partially boxed at the key stress points in keeping with the Kennedy plan. They don't go the super heavy-duty route unless big power is going to be applied, and big-inch modern power is not really their bag anyway. Using genuine rails is just one of the ways the Kennedys keep everything as original as possible. On this car, there is a little extra bracing due to the mild 327-ci Chevy and T-5 trans. Such a powertrain is not the norm for the Kennedys, but this customer specified the combo for long-distance cruising. In keeping with the highway theme, a set of anti-rollbars complements the otherwise original suspension. The all-steel body received a mellow 2 1/2-inch chop, and the interior is getting a "French" dash fabbed by Soliday. Lance also spotted in some primer to match the original patina and handled the wiring, as well as a lot of the assembly.

This roadster is the definition of "less is more." This total highboy has no dropped axle, employing classic big 'n' littles for the perfect stance. The Ford 25-louver hood sides hide a 283-ci 'Vette motor with two four-barrels generating 270 horsepower. Jimmy Shine is responsible for the chassis, and the boys swear this is the last one they'll "paint nice." Gabe's Upholstery did the interior and top.

51

Now you know what a true hot rod candy shop really looks like. This is the "rec room" at the Kennedy shop.

This Phaeton is ready to move, thanks to the McCulloch-blown 59A flathead. The old KH wires set it off nicely. Joe Kennedy Sr. wood-grained the dash and Carol Knapp did the tonneau and upholstery.

The other car under construction at the shop is going to be a mindblower clone of a car the Kennedys thought was real cool. They took the idea to Jard, who went along with the project. The frame is finished and detailed to the nines, wearing a royal blue coat of paint; a chromed rear axle and chromed tube shocks spice the deal up a little bit. The entire front suspension is also chrome. Between the rails sits a fully detailed 354-ci Hemi painted copper with chrome covers and chromed cast-iron exhaust manifolds. The body is a three-window Ford coupe, of course. The car being cloned was known as *The Devil Deuce* when it came out in the early '50s. It was a wild ride with Hemi power and Satan emblazoned across the grille shell for all to see.

The Kennedys have been working the hot rod thing professionally since the early 1990s to get where they are today. When they first started, they built or modified anything they could get their hands on. Now they stick pretty much to deuces because it's where the market puts its money. According to Joe, "The '32 is a good hot rod out of the box."

For the underlying philosophy and method to the madness, it's best to go straight to the source. "A few years ago, we did a roadster that was in *Rod & Custom*," Joe explains. "The car came from Australia. It was folded up in a box. We put it all back together. The customer wanted to make it all nice and we were like, no, let's make a beater out of it. So I put one coat of black

paint on it with red oxide underneath and buffed it through. Another car we did, the customer wanted to paint and we said no way. It's got great old primer on it. So we did the chassis real nice, did the engine real nice, detailed the drivetrain, and put the old body on it like it had been there a long time. These cars were like a turning point for us. Prior to that, it had been all nice paint jobs and now we're just sick of them. We try to use as much original stuff as we can. We'll modify other stuff. There's more satisfaction in that than using something that's off the shelf."

Under the skin, according to Joe, the Kennedy Brothers' cars are "all set up pretty much the same way. We've got a formula. If you are running a flathead, we mate that with a '39 trans and a '36 rear axle, dropped front end, tube shocks, and '56 steering. You gotta modify everything a bit, but it works; it's the right combo. Simplicity is the key. Sometimes we mix in some Chevy 283-ci or 327-ci. Chevy is about all we'll use 'cause you don't have to cut everything up; they bolt right in with an adapter. We're just hung up on simplicity."

Even keeping it simple, the brothers and Lance manage two completes a year with a little small stuff on the side. It takes time and hard work to maintain the quality the Kennedy Brothers' rides are known for, and a rush job or a quality compromise just isn't in the cards. A Kennedy Brothers ride is traditional, well built, and aesthetically spot-on.

This '32 five-window started it all for the Kennedy Brothers—it was the first car they built with the intention of selling. Originally a basket case, it was turned into a clean traditional piece powered by a '49 8BA flathead with Offy heads and a twin 97 intake. The frame is a genuine '32, and Carol Knapp did the upholstery.

Mercury Charlie

South Austin Speed Shop

Charlie in his "wild" years, posing with two of his namesakes. At one time he owned 16 Mercs.

SOUTH AUSTIN SPEED SHOT OPENED ITS DOORS IN OCTOBER OF 2005.

Five principle investors—Dr. Dan Peterson, Cory Moore, John Joyoprayitno, Mercury Charlie Runnels, and Sean Johnstun—pooled their resources and love of old cars to create a true one-stop facility for vintage-car enthusiasts. Any and all manner of custom fabrication, assembly, chassis work, repair, and completes down to custom-stitched upholstery are done in-house. Mercury Charlie is the hundred-mile-an-hour sage on the buildup side of the business, and relative youngster Sean Johnstun is the mad genius behind the evolving custom upholstery side called Fat Lucky's. Charlie has a crew of three, including Wade Munson, Mike Ramirez, and apprentice Chris Gee. Sean does his thing with apprentice Dave Mandujano. Both Sean and Charlie worked out of their homes before the shop opened.

The shop building was constructed in 1959 by a B-29 bomber mechanic who had an auto repair business. It is a large, airy affair with plenty of room for everyone to play together nicely. There is a generous amount of dirt out back and to the side to keep a well-stocked boneyard, and on any given day upward of five cars are getting work done. The shop also features a glassed-in office/receiving area that houses a very special '51 chopped Mercury custom called *Nadine* that belongs to Mercury Charlie. The story of South Austin Speed Shop begins with Charlie—and Charlie's story is one of scrappy hard work and the 20 years of his life he dedicated to the building of *Nadine*.

The thing about Charlie is his irrepressibility. Animated is too weak a word to describe him, and manic perhaps too severe. He is full-on all the time. Hands are moving, at once providing punctuation and then lighting another of the omnipresent cigarettes he smokes. He pauses for breath but only for emphasis, and while he tells his stories, he makes direct eye contact and is genuinely excited. Almost childlike in his enthusiasm, it is clear that Charlie has a true love for car culture in particular, and 1950s postwar American culture in general. His stories are as tall as a two-lane blacktop is long and they are legendary.

This '59 Chevrolet El Camino was the first complete in-house car for South Austin Speed Shop. A real tough nut, the car came in with no floor from "your toes to the tailgate," as Charlie puts it. The car has Air Ride, its original 348-ci power plant, a smoothed firewall, and in-house fender-well covers to hide the suspension. Sean Johnstun did the interior in a classic late-'50s/early-'60s motif. Mike Ramirez came in and took care of some of the mechanical details, hid the AC, and got the motor runnin'.

"I didn't really have parents when I was a kid," Charlie begins. "My mom died at an early age. I lived with everybody in the family. At the age of 14, I had a newspaper route, had some other jobs, and with some help from my brother bought a '64 Chevrolet Impala with the 327 and a Muncie four-speed. I didn't have a driver's license yet. I ran away to Oklahoma City. I went to the high school and said 'I'm here to go to school.' I sat down with the counselor and told him my situation and they got me a job flippin' pancakes. The only place I could afford for rent was on the wrong side of the tracks for a white boy to be at. I met this older Indian guy there that had a Phillips 66 gas station. By workin' for him for free, I finally got him to let me use the wrecker on Saturdays and Sundays.

"I started noticing all these '55 and '56 Chevrolets around the neighborhood. I'd go door to door and if the lady of the house was there I'd say, 'Ma'am, if you've got two dollars and the title of that car, I'll haul that off for ya,' and sometimes it worked. I am haulin' cars to this Indian's gas station as fast as I can haul 'em. I take all the good stuff out of the car and sell the rest for scrap metal, and now I've got change to make it through the week and I'm not havin' to work a part-time job. I'm doin' more and more. I'm taking all these parts and stockpiling. I finally work my way to a '55 Chevrolet that was so close to the *Two-Lane Blacktop* car. I went to that movie in a car that was close. I got a '55 Chevrolet with a 427 moved back into the car with 12.5:1 pop-ups. A fiberglass lift-off front end. Straight axle and no front brakes. Glass doors and Plexiglas windows with a leather strap on 'em. Two glass buckets and fiberglass deck lid. I'm running moonshine 50-50 with aviation fuel. My goal is that every muscle car that's on the list that's the hot one of the day, I'm gonna beat it."

His dogged determination stayed with Charlie through life's ups and downs. Cars never left him and at one time he had 16 Mercurys, but only the very special one is still with him today—the car he calls *Nadine*.

"*Nadine* was started 20-some odd years ago," Charlie explains. "It was a labor of love and a major disease. This car was an abandoned vehicle that the government paid me $165 to haul off a piece of property. I said, 'I'm keeping this one.' I rolled the odometer to zero and I drove the car for five years and put 49,000 miles on it...this motor this transmission."

After Charlie Sexton blew up first gear, Mercury Charlie put the car away in his back yard. One day Sexton came over with his guitar. "He got in the car and he sat down and he played 'Mercury Blues' for me," Charlie remembers.

"Shortly after that I said, 'I'm gonna build my dream. I'm gonna have the same motto as Duesenberg had during the Depression.' At the height of the Depression, they said, 'Damn the cost,' so I kinda went on this theory. The day I tore the car apart, I did this," Charlie says, showing his tattoo of the Mercury logo. "If I do this and I take a shower or I'm shaving, I'm gonna look like an idiot if I sell the car and I don't finish this. So I started the process on the car. Every part on here is either a Lincoln or a Mercury part spanning '49 to '58. Gary Howard has a tremendous amount of influence on it, but I still had some things where I wanted to go even past Gary with. Gary's idea on frenching the headlights different from everybody else was phenomenal. Normally everybody welds the '54 ring on and that's it. This one has been dropped and pulled out. The fender now has a different curve than everybody else's. I wanted the

A corner of the South Austin Speed Shop lounge area featuring Mecury Charlie wall art.

Charlie's hands caught at 1/500th of a second.

"Mercury" Charlie

TEXAS '591 HF·3341

WA·

'51 grille, but I wanted inset like the '50 or '49 grille. Gary and I cut up I don't know how many grilles. We made the front bumper out of four bumpers. It didn't work out and we got four more bumpers and did it again. I threw over 20K worth of chrome away. Rejects. We took all the seams out of the car. Everything's been done in lead. I wanted it to look like the factory coulda done it."

Nadine's motor has a Bonneville and Kong Jackson influence. Charlie tells how it happened: "First of all, we went to all the car shows out in California. Lookin' at flathead after flathead and all the Mercs and tryin' to figure out how I can beat the big dogs at their own game. I seen flatheads with three deuces, two deuces, four deuces—nothing changes. But if I go back and look at the Bonneville stuff, especially if you look back on some of the stuff that Kong did.... My buddy, Roach [Billy Cockrell], actually got a hold of Kong to see if anything was available. Nothin' was, so Roach drew this up [the six-sidedraft-carb manifold], went into a computer, did a few things on the computer, and said it'd work. He milled out the bottom plate with fins on it as per my instructions. I wanted it to have a feel kinda like the heads."

The manifold is beautiful and the runners are mandrel bent tubing. "Roach designed it," Charlie continues. "Roach made the pieces; I take the pieces home and polish 'em. Roach welds 'em up; I bring it back and polish it over and over again 'til the whole damn thing was done. The upper radiator tubes are from Roach. There are 2,264 checkers on the block. It took a long to time to figure out how to do it." The checkers pass over the block at an angle and the motor sat so long in the house that the white on the checkers yellowed and it had to be done again. "Like I said," Charlie says, "a lot of the parts on the car, we'd make it, get it done, put it on the car, and if it wasn't right, we threw it away and we'd do it again. I'm broke, I'm poor, I don't care. It's gonna take me an insane amount of time, but the car's got to be right.

"There's still some things on the car I'm gonna get back into. We rounded the back of the hood, but look at the way Gary did all that and the inside of the firewall. I watched all this go down, and to see what he did, and how it all worked out, boggles my mind. Gary Howard is a voodoo guy when it comes to this stuff. Look at everybody who does it and look at the back side and you'll be able to see what they did. Not the way Gary does it. Gary chopped the roof and he pancaked the roof to keep the lines over the quarter glass in proportion. If chopping the top is brain surgery, then what he did was brair

This is *Nadine*, the 1951 Mercury dream car that Charlie envisioned and which Gary Howard built and painted. The car has rack-and-pinion steering and air bags and retains its stock column. The headliner is a one-piece inset, and Vernon McKean made every button in the interior by hand over the course of two months. The '58 Lincoln Premier factory-option-only hubcaps are made even more unique by the addition of 37-ounce stainless-steel soup ladles for centers. That rear window is also '51, by the way.

surgery and a heart transplant all on one roof. From underside the roof, you can tell that it was cut, but just barely. There's no grind marks! Then he skimmed the whole thing in lead. I think four bars into it. Drip rails have been shaved, the B-pillar tilted forward. The front of the door has been rounded. There is not a 90-degree anywhere. We even rounded the corners on the glove-box door. I think he sprayed 37 coats of lacquer. A lot of people brag about their car, but we went beyond the nth degree. I tried to do that with every single thing on this car."

The incredible amount of time and expense involved in building *Nadine* might have you wondering how a hot rodding, poor-boy locksmith from Oklahoma could pull it off. In true Mercury Charlie fashion, there is an incredible story here as well. With a roll of his eyes and a big drag off a smoke, he tells it: "Doing *Nadine* just drained me. I mortgaged the house, the girlfriend, everything. I emptied the Neiderwald [Texas] salvage yard. The guy was kinda wacky, but he liked me. I made keys for him for free, so he gave me carte blanche. I was the only guy that was ever allowed to drive into the salvage yard. It was 20-some odd acres. The newest car was '62 or '3. If you stood on top of the hill in the middle of Cadillac row, it went in both directions. About as far as your little eyes could see was Cadillacs. When he told me that he had some trouble with the IRS he said, 'Everything you can drag out of here is yours for free.' I hauled a '55 Lincoln Capri out. I hauled out three Buick Rivieras. One that was in a building, I had to make a line for the wrecker to get to it and when I got to it, there was a crate I couldn't move on top of it that said General Motors. Cracked it open, 425 Buick engine, from the factory, in the crate. The '63 Buick Riviera behind it had every amenity that you could check off for on a Riviera in '63. Then we went out there with two pickups and two trailers, two acetylene torches and five men, and two weeks. We started at the beginning of Cadillac row. This was all for *Nadine*, this is what happened. We started at the bottom of the hill, and worked our way over the hill and back the other side in one week. We put plywood down to knock thegrass down around the back and around the front of the car. I had guys taking a screwdriver and hammer

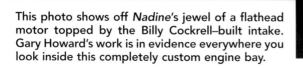

This photo shows off *Nadine*'s jewel of a flathead motor topped by the Billy Cockrell–built intake. Gary Howard's work is in evidence everywhere you look inside this completely custom engine bay.

Trucks getting a rusty fade in the South Austin Speed Shop boneyard include (left to right) a '57 International, a '53 Studebaker, and a '50 Chevy.

and popping the trunk lock and emptying the contents out. I start on the rear of the car and another friend of mine with a torch in the front. We'd light our torches when the sun came up and we started cutting. I'd cut a rear end off and he's cuttin' the front end off. We have no time. I'm crying. We go back at nightfall with the pickups and the trailers bulging. Go to my backyard and stack, go back, and get more. When I closed the gate at the end of two weeks, the back door to my house, I could open it and that's it. To do *Nadine* and be a poor man and go, 'Damn the cost,' I got lucky. There was a guy from Germany came up from Houston in a huge truck to my house and he'd fill the truck and take it back to a container and send that to Germany. And he kept comin' back and doin' it until he emptied my back yard. That's how I afforded a lot of *Nadine*."

Nadine was a crazy labor of love for Charlie and everyone involved, and it sure paid off. She's a unique and beautiful custom done in the traditional vein whose design characteristics will stay fresh forever because she was done right. When it comes to flavor-of-the-moment hot rods, Charlie is characteristically outspoken. As he tells this one, he gets a bit more heated and leans in for his points. "These cats build a car with these big wheels, billet aluminum, and all that, and you look back to the trends of 1975, '85, '95, and now, you're following in the footsteps of all these guys back here," he says. "You've built a car that's out of time, out of date, and you've got to rebuild the car. There's all these talented guys out there and they've all lost one ingredient: style.

"How can you take an '80s Camaro mirror and put it on your '30s car? Would you buy a Victorian home and modernize it? Would you wear a tuxedo and Bermuda shorts to a big event? These are fashion faux pas and we have no fashion police in this car world goin', 'You guys are fuckin' up! Somebody, please pull the plug!' Then I have people tellin' me, 'We're doin' it because everything's already been done.' Well, that's no excuse."

Instead of leaving it at that, he offers a solution for the would-be rodder or customizer. Clearly relishing his subject matter, Charlie lays it out: "When you see the [designers' sketches for the] Holy Grail vehicle, they never made that car. But as time went by, there's a part of it on a Cadillac. There's a piece on a Chevrolet. Take that idea and work it backwards. Pick your favorite car and go either direction in a five- to seven-year span picking parts that work tastefully with your car and you've just built a dream car in reverse." Charlie might not be the first to voice this concept, but he puts it so eloquently and with so much conviction that it bears inclusion.

When Charlie speaks about dream cars and customs, he is referring to post–World War II American culture. A time period he holds in high esteem. "The culture that we had after World War II up until the time Buddy Holly died was so unique, so magic," he explains. "None of that can ever happen again. That's why it's so sought after, it's so unique. People from all over the world, they wanna buy vintage guitars, cars, dresses, blue jeans, you name it. Because what happened in America after the war was that we were only influenced from the inside. Every single part of America at that time was not pulled from over here and over there. It's our own melting pot of our own culture. What I'm leading to is that that was a nondisposable world. You bought stuff and it lasted you for long, long periods of time. If you walk into some cat's house and he's got a stack of vinyl, a record player, an old blender, old plates, old silverware, old toaster, maybe a Wurlitzer jukebox. When that cat dies, the line of people that are gonna fight for everything in that house is really long. Most everybody else, when they die, the aunt and uncle go in and say, 'Do you want this or should we throw it away?' What kind of life was that? That most of the stuff you had in your house—that you had as surroundings—is disposable garbage? Everybody's trained today: 'Buy it, use it, throw it away.' But not these cars we're playing with, not these guitars musicians are seeking out, not the

A '56 Cadillac and an ultrarare '51 Mercury convertible wait their turn under the Texas sun.

vinyl, not the furniture, any of that stuff. People are gonna fight for it until it's all in museums and nobody can have it."

What South Austin Speed Shop is building and striving for is nondisposability; cars that won't need to be redone in five years' time. It is a serious undertaking that requires the right frame of mind. Charlie has his own ideas about how and who to hire on. "I didn't get paid to go work on cars as a kid. I had to fight the old guys to learn," he says. "After I fought hard enough, they'd give me a half a tank of gas. When we got our apprentice, Dave Mandujano, here for upholstery, we told him, 'You come down here for three months and work for free and put your nose to the grindstone and if we like what you're doing, then we'll hire you.' I'm not hiring people that say, 'I wanna be'; I'm hiring people that are gonna fight. If you're fightin' tooth and nail like I had to do as a kid to get in here, then I know you're comin' from the right place. If you're showin' up here for a paycheck, you're not it. Go punch your clock, go get your eight hours and dream of what you're gonna do and never accomplish it. I have to have people that are gonna go the extra, extra step with everything. That's why I wanted Sean to be a business partner. Whatever it takes, he's gonna get it done. He's gonna get it done with great taste and great talent."

As Charlie walks through the shop he grins and says, "You wanna ask me, 'Why do you do this?' Some people go to work every day. I come here to my playhouse every day. I think Pete Chapouris might have said it first: 'When I'm in my car and I'm goin' down the road, I'm 20 years old.' When I'm driving my car, you can't beat the smile off of me. When I'm workin' on the car, I'm working with the metal and working with a piece of equipment that'll surpass me and the next generation. People will keep wanting this stuff. It's nondisposable. It's a magic thing that we're getting to do here. Getting to this means all the aches and pains of years of 15- and 18-hour days go away to an extent because I'm playing with some of the coolest stuff. I couldn't dream a better thing to do. I'm not going to work, punching a clock, working in a cubicle. I get to work on something that'll be here when I'm dead and gone. You look underneath the dash on my cars and they're all signed with my name and the date that I did 'em."

Vast expanse of shop space is revealed in this view (a good one-third is obscured to the left). The shop El Camino project is in the foreground; behind it is a '63 Riviera in for a "Fat Lucky" interior, and on the lift is another Mercury.

Sean Johnstun with the frontseat he designed for the shop '59 El Camino.

A Fat Lucky combo platter of Naugahyde, glitter roll, and western-inspired pinstriping.

ONE HALF OF SOUTH AUSTIN SPEED SHOP IS THE PRODIGIOUSLY TALENTED SEAN JOHNSTUN

(the other half being Mercury Charlie). The hot rod and custom world has seen the likes of such great trimmers as Tony Nancy, Sid Chavers, and Vernon McKeane. Now there is a new talent on the scene who is not only producing great-looking, well-thought-out upholstery, but is also an innovator and trendsetter.

Sean came out of the suburban sprawl of Las Vegas. Under the hot sun, car culture reigned supreme in Sean's neighborhood, but it was not hot rod culture at all. Latino-influenced low rider culture was the "in" scene among Sean and his friends. Sean cut his teeth doing tuck-and-roll after tuck-and-roll on Impalas and the like. Skate and snowboard cultures also had their play in his development. He was obviously talented, and after high school he set out for a year of fashion design school in San Francisco.

Sean is a quiet man with a head full of ideas. With a little coaxing, he tells the story of how he grew up and how Fat Lucky's Upholstery came to be. He starts off slowly and then settles in. "I was a skater/punk rock kid," he begins. "Me and my little group of rebellious friends. I started makin' my own clothes in high school; I started sellin' stuff in skateboard and snowboard shops. I wanted to have a little sportswear company. This was early '90s. The more I got into the industry, I could tell it was not the place for me. And I got really frustrated with the school because I had already been teaching myself all this stuff for a few years and the school was just going so slow that I started skipping and teaching myself at home. Pretty soon I was like, 'What am I doing here?' All the guys my age were into low riders. I was like eighteen or nineteen. And everybody said, 'Well, you make all these clothes, can you do my interior?' I was like, 'Yeah, bring it on.' I like low riders, but I like hot rods and customs, but that was like old guys. I got a lot of older guys telling me, 'You're too young. You haven't been doin' this long enough.' So I worked on a lot of Impalas. I only did a couple of cars that were really crazy, like button-tufted custom things. But it's all pretty much the same thing I'm doin'now. I learned from taking stuff apart and seeing how it's put together. Fortunately, the first couple of cars I did hadn't been reupholstered by anyone else so I got to take apart the factory stuff and see how things are really supposed to be put together. I try to keep it all as nice underneath as it is on the top. I don't want any other upholstery guy to take this apart in the future and just think I hacked it together. Even though this is something that nobody's ever gonna see, except for me.

"That got me into doin' this," Sean continues. "That was about 10 years ago when I moved here. The first person I met out here was Charlie, as far as getting into the car scene. I lived in the same neighborhood as him and I would see him working on cars all the time, and I stopped by one day and I brought my little portfolio and asked him if he needed \any interior work done. He didn't even look at my book. He was like, 'Yeah, I need a helluva lot done. How much do you want for 'em?' A lot of the car scene I know in Austin is one way or another through Charlie. We eventually opened up a shop together."

Sean's foundation in the low rider interiors, clothes design, and paying close attention to good design in general is backed by his own set of influences. At the same time, the ideas for his designs just seem to be coming out of his head all the time. In that respect, he is like any other driven artist. "The time I spend [building, stitching, and covering] something might take two or three

Pleated, plain, and pinstriped custom solo motorcycle seats by Sean.

Above: A beautifully understated Fat Lucky interior graces a '63 Riviera.

Left: Sean did the neat trim job on the cockpit of Gary Fegley's '29 Ford roadster pickup.

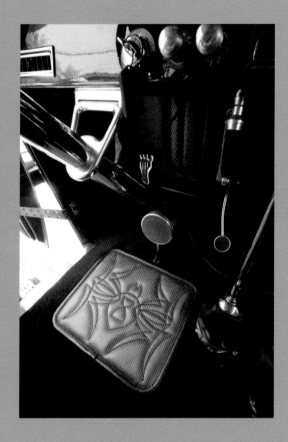

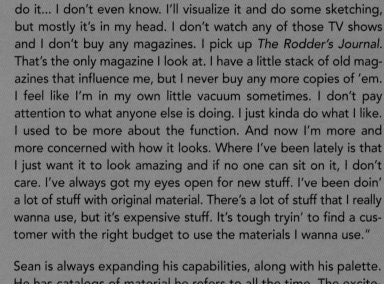

These spiderweb motifs are among the very first pin-stripe stylings stitched by Sean Johnstun.

This diamond-pleated pickup bedcover with pin-stripe motif is bound for a Gary Howard–painted pickup.

days," he explains, "but the time I spend thinking about how to do it... I don't even know. I'll visualize it and do some sketching, but mostly it's in my head. I don't watch any of those TV shows and I don't buy any magazines. I pick up *The Rodder's Journal*. That's the only magazine I look at. I have a little stack of old magazines that influence me, but I never buy any more copies of 'em. I feel like I'm in my own little vacuum sometimes. I don't pay attention to what anyone else is doing. I just kinda do what I like. I used to be more about the function. And now I'm more and more concerned with how it looks. Where I've been lately is that I just want it to look amazing and if no one can sit on it, I don't care. I've always got my eyes open for new stuff. I've been doin' a lot of stuff with original material. There's a lot of stuff that I really wanna use, but it's expensive stuff. It's tough tryin' to find a customer with the right budget to use the materials I wanna use."

Sean is always expanding his capabilities, along with his palette. He has catalogs of material he refers to all the time. The excitement he shows as he pores over the pages is genuine. Another discipline he approached was furniture-making, and he tells how it came about and the part it plays in his automotive work. "I live in a project house," he explains. "Anything outside of my car projects is my house project. I have enough crazy stuff goin' on in my head that I need to go home to someplace nice and calm. I really like a modern, superbasic, stripped-down style. A lot of the auto upholstery I do is probably a lot flashier than some of the furniture stuff I'm into. It's probably still a big influence. I used to build modern furniture stuff. For a while, I was contracted to build headboards and benches and stuff and they had me covering stuff with Ultrasuede and from there I started doing headliners out of Ultrasuede. I started bringin' all that stuff into the cars. And the other way around, I did a bunch of cool furniture stuff using wacky automotive vinyls."

This willingness to cross-pollinate also paid off when Sean combined pinstriping with his upholstery. We are not talking about appliqués here—these original pinstripe designs are physically stitched into the material. Sean started with spiderweb-themed designs, and then around 2001 he worked up his own abstractions that can call to mind swallows' wings or the fins of graceful fish. Mercury Charlie enjoys telling the story of how he took a Cadillac that Sean had done for him years ago over to Vernon McKeane. Vern looked at the upholstery and said, "Damn, how old is the guy that did this?" Charlie told him that Sean was 24 years old at the time and Vern said, "You're kidding me. If I was doin' this upholstery when I was 24, I would've retired a lot earlier."

Returning the compliment Sean says, "For a long time, I haven't really been very impressed with anybody except for Vern's stuff. I still look at some of his stuff and I can't figure out how he did it. It's cool to have him come here and say stuff like that to me, too. When I first started doing this pinstriping stuff he was starin' at it for a long time and he was like, 'How do you do that?' It's cool to hear stuff like that from somebody I really respect."

You might wonder how Sean came up with the name Fat Lucky's for his business. He is happy to tell. "I got the name from my dog—a little fat beagle. Fat Lucky was just his nickname and I ended up naming my business after him. Now it's just a source of confusion for everybody 'cause I'm obviously not fat and everybody wants to know why I'm called Fat Lucky. It was just the name of the business and then everybody just started calling me Fat Lucky. Lucky passed away five years ago." That beagle's name will be remembered for a very long time, thanks to Sean's impeccable, innovative work.

You have not seen the last of Fat Lucky's Upholstery, or of Sean Johnstun. "Each car I do is getting better and better," he states. The designs just get wilder and wilder, and Sean constantly tops himself. Just when you think you've got the coolest Fat Lucky interior, Sean ups the ante on the next one. And you'd better get in line because, as Sean says, "I'm booked up for the rest of my life."

This nice traditional Model A five-window is accented by a tuxedo tuck-and-roll with pinstripe-accented Fat Lucky interior.

Keith Tardel

Rex Rod & Chassis

W

ALKING THROUGH THE FRONT DOOR OF KEITH TARDEL'S REX ROD & CHASSIS ONLY GIVES AWAY SO MUCH ABOUT WHAT LIES BEYOND THE SMALL ROOM YOU'VE JUST ENTERED.

On the walls there are a few photos, a couple of posters, and a David Peters print of Larry "Jungle" Faust entitled *Bakersfield Blues*. There is a window dead ahead and peering through it reveals an engine-assembly room. There are doors to the right and left.

Go through door number one on the right and try not to walk into a fully detailed flathead that is ready to run on the test stand. When Keith fires it up, it barks and then purrs away, the note echoing around the first of three large rooms. The corrugated tin walls are a carnival of vintage signage, automobilia, a frame-rail rack, and a multitude of parts. Farther down the line, a Bridgeport mill, drill press, and blast cabinet await their work.

On the chassis table, there is a '32 Tudor. Keith boxed the rails using plates cut from the outside of the rails to provide the same reveal on the inner as well as the outer rail. The radius rods are drilled and filled all the way down the taper. They look absolutely perfect, and when asked how long it took to get them so nice, Keith lets out the kind of groan that says, "Forever." A 392 Hemi with a Richmond five-speed will provide ample motivation. The top is coming down soon and the wheelwells are being moved to preserve proportion. When finished, the car will sport a mid-'60s vibe and detail indicative of the work you can expect from Rex Rod.

The ceiling is barking with a late May rain and a '40 Ford coupe is undergoing some corrective surgery. The coupe first came to Keith as a restored car. He sectioned it 2 inches, chopped it an inch, and channeled it 4 inches. He put in a full cage and all the necessary gear to make 9-second passes. The car did what it was built to do, until it gave the guardrail a smooch. Now it is here in the shop to be brought back to life as a street car.

A Bonneville record trophy commemorates the 2002 record set by the '27 T built by Keith and driven by Larry Mackenzie.

Next to the '40 coupe is a '30 Ford five-window belonging to Ryan Cochrane of jalopyjournal.com This car is in for a very traditional post-war hot rod treatment. Aftermarket frame rails are employed, but Keith has drilled out all the old mounting points for a genuine barn-fresh look. Keith has already done the 2-inch chop and it looks dead-on. All early Ford running gear and a flathead will take the car down the road. The body will stay where Henry put it, on top of the rails, and KH wire rims and bias plies will complete the traditional picture.

Walking past Ryan's '30 and some stray flatties brings you to another world within the world of Rex Rods. Again, the walls are in full dress. Speedway and drag strip posters advertise high-speed thrills on straights and ovals that are long paved over by strip malls and cul-de-sacs. Many of the posters have been cleverly manipulated to include Rex Rods somewhere in the text.

The main event on this day is a rare '36 club cabriolet that was bought at an auction in nearly all-original condition. Juice brakes, a drop axle, and a 59A flathead with a 3/8 Potvin cam are going in on the hop-up installment plan. Sitting low in the background is a stock '56 Lincoln. On a couple of dollies sits Keith's next personal project: a Brookville '32 roadster. All those little ol' molecules in that steel must be staring at the shiny '36 and then over at the major surgery next door and wondering what sort of fate awaits them. The fate that does await is a true '40s-style highboy with a little speed equipment. Keith says, "It's a dream car, so I want to take some time on it and hopefully keep it." It seems Keith is no stranger to the court of sentiment vs. money.

Back in the main room, behind the bench behind the wall, is Keith's well-appointed parts room. Just about all you need, from bumpers to

Mike Hawes came up with this through-the-fender exhaust that Keith executed.

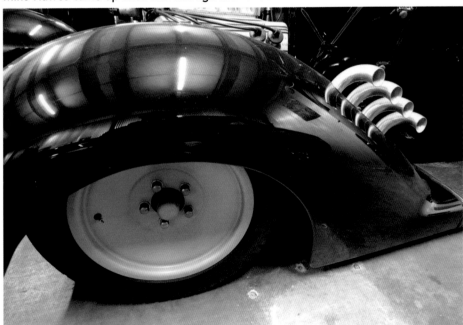

A blown, injected Ardun powers the Rex-built chopped '36 three-window. In the background is a '62 Ford Galaxie Holman Moody exhibition car built to show off the new-for-'62 406-ci three-deuce motors.

A chopped '32 Tudor is on the chassis table while an ex-racer '40 Ford sits in the background. Just visible behind it is a '30 Ford coupe under construction for Ryan Cochrane.

transmissions, is there in plain view for easy pickins. Banjo rears are lined up like pinky rings in a giant's jewelry box. And hanging on the wall is the louvered steel Christmas stocking Keith made for his wife, Mary. Off to the side is the bare-bones office. It's exactly what you'd expect in a place where most of the action is of the truly hands-on type.

In the third room are Paul Boschetto's car collection and the tiki clubhouse. In the center of the room is the '34 roadster Keith built that was in the beauty ring at the 2006 San Francisco Rod and Custom Show. The old real steel body sits on an original '34 frame. The lack of running boards reveals how the body drapes just over the frame rail, as if it has been ever so slightly channeled. The stance is right and the Thickstun-equipped 296-ci flathead takes its drink through two Stromberg 97s. Keith gave the car a polished-yet-bare-bones look with upholstery from school bus stock.

For fans of Ford NASCAR history, the third room also features a Holman Moody "promo" car. The '62 Galaxie is lettered like the real thing, but the only real hardware it packs is the new-for-'62, 406-ci tri-power motor. Stealing a bit of thunder from the Galaxie is a horror-movie evil '36 Ford three-window. Like Mike Hawes' original rendering for the coupe, it features zoomies up through the fenders. Blowing a sweet song out those pipes is a blown and injected Ardun. Keith built this one top to bottom and also found a set of magnesium Halibrands that set off the car perfectly.

Just to cement Paul's rep as a Ford nut, there is a 427-powered re-pop AC Cobra, a 427-powered '64 Galaxie, and the real heavy hitter, a 1940 Lincoln Zephyr. This baby is nearly all original and the V-12 flathead and mohair upholstery in the neckin' nook behind the front seat are both clamoring for a workout.

Keith dives into the nearly bone-stock '36 Ford Club Cabriolet. To spice things up just a little, a drop axle and a 59A motor with 3/8 Potvin cam are going in. On the lift in the background is a '56 Lincoln.

These cars, the art on the walls, and the go-kart dragster lead back to the aforementioned tin hut. The blue neon flashing "BAR" over the front door calls your name. Two floral upholstered, bamboo-framed easy chairs flank the door like doormen inviting you inside. Inside, the walls are thatched, the art is Hawaiian, and the view out the window is pure hot rod. The bar is in diamond-themed bamboo and it's stocked. A marlin arcs over the hula lamp–lit back bar, while tiki-style pin-ups vie for attention with every kind of tiki-style carving, lighting, and primitivo sculpture imaginable. A cheesecake painting features a reckless driver, some cops, and the cause of it all is about to take off her top. This place is about as close as you can get to true "mantopia." This room is also where Keith told his story.

Keith's father is Vern Tardel, the talented and longtime builder of traditionally flavored hot rods. Keith says Vern's influence came from just being around his dad. Of his first exposure to hot rods, Keith recalls, "After school, I'd go to the body shop and sweep floors or sort nuts and bolts." There is no doubt that Keith was learning more than how to tell the difference between a grade 5 and a grade 8 bolt. Consciously or unconsciously, he was absorbing an aesthetic and a work ethic that emphasized pride in craft and hard work. When Vern bought Keith a quarter-midget racer, the deal was sealed. "I guess that's what set me off," Keith says.

The midget led to a '64 Ford Falcon set up for the drag strip. Keith leans across the rattan bar and reflects, "I built that car in my senior year. I put a 429 together on a limited budget and had a lot of fun with it. I gained a lot of knowledge and had help from people who'd been around it all their lives, like Ron Frye." In the end, bracket racing held less and less appeal for Keith.

Around 1993, "I got into sprint cars," Keith continues, "helping a buddy with 360-ci sprint cars." Getting in deeper, Keith began to shed possessions:

erating, rather than constraining. It meant being creative, resourceful, and getting things right the first time.

Eventually the racing was "consuming" Keith's life. He "had to build a hot rod. I was done with the racing thing." Pausing for a pull on a cold beer, Keith resumes his story. "I remember going over to my dad's shop. I sat down and said, 'I think I'm gonna build a hot rod.' And Vern said, 'Oh, OK.' I told him I was gonna build a '29 roadster pickup and he says, 'Oh, I think I have an axle out back.'" The room fills with a laugh and then Keith remarks in a more serious tone that Vern "pretty much stood back, just to see if it was a phase or whatever. But I was set."

Keith built the truck, just as he had envisioned it, on '32 rails and with flathead power. The body came one piece at a time from Brookville and Keith assembled it bit by newly arrived bit, honing his fit and finish skills in the process. The body went in primer and stayed that way. Family friend Ed Dalpoggetto remembers

Cochrane's '30 Ford coupe after its 2-inch chop, and the '40 Ford waiting for its new life on the street.

Tiki hut interior

Paul Boschetto's auto play land includes the tiki hut and, from left to right, a 427 AC Cobra, the Holman Moody Galaxie, a '34 Ford roadster, the '36 coupe, the 427-powered '64 Galaxie, and a 1940 Lincoln Zephyr.

the day Keith first drove the truck. "I'll never forget when that little truck started movin' on its own," Ed says. "I was sittin' on a running board with Vern, and Vern was just like a proud papa."

Keith was pretty excited to be motoring the truck and recalls, "When I first put the bed on it, it had no windshield, no plates, no nothin'. I went to take it out about a mile and a half. I was thinkin', 'This thing feels really good.' I wound up all the way in Healdsburg. I was having a great time and I knew then that was probably a determining moment. I said to myself, 'I've screwed around with all this other stuff. I'm gonna build hot rods.'"

At the time the pickup was being built, Keith was locksmithing to pay the bills. Vern noticed Keith's talent for building and suggested that Keith work with him at the shop. "I thought about it and I felt it was time for a change, and I started working for him full-time," Keith says. He got as much out of the experience as he could. Working side by side with his dad "was good. It was great experience. We did a lot of cars there and I did at least three completes on my own." The people he worked with, along with his dad, run down like a who's who of NoCal hot rodding. "Talk about getting knowledge," Keith says. "Kent Fuller was there. Gary Camara, Terry Griffith, Ed Binggeli, Mike Bishop. We had a rare pool of people. Everyone had their own specialty, but if need be, they could figure out anything."

Keith first started getting into body mods on a '32 three-window that had already been chopped. "The back [of the roof] was pretty good, but the front was unfinished," Keith says. "Kent Fuller took a Skilsaw and cut a section out of the pillar and handed it to me. He said, 'You need to reshape that and put it back in' and then he just walked away. I said, 'OK, great.' That car was a first for me." It sounds like trial by fire, but it also speaks to the trust Kent had in Keith's ability to solve the problem.

Keith started getting so good that Vern couldn't stay ahead with the motors he was building for the cars. But Keith modestly says that there is no mystery to it all. "There are certain formulas and certain combinations," he explains. "You just get to the point where, if you have everything there, you can get it done in a couple of days. It's not rocket science. It's simplicity at its best."

Above: This '34 roadster is an old Steve's Restorations body on an original '34 frame with a '39 transmission and a '46 rear end. The traditional rod is powered by a 296-ci flathead with Sharp heads and a Thickstun PM-7 intake with two Stromberg 97s. The perfect highboy stance comes from 5x16 Firestones up front, 7.5x16 Firestones out back, and a 3-inch drop axle. Paintwork credit goes to Eddie Serrano; Eric Sadletzky did the pinstriping.

Right: An interior shot shows the '40 Ford dash and steering wheel, the 2-inch cut on the stock windscreen, and the "school bus" Naugahyde upholstery.

Even though Keith had foresworn race cars, a visit to Bonneville inspired him and friend Larry Mackenzie to build a hot rod for the salt. Larry said to Keith, "Hey, I've got the money, you know how to do it, let's build a car." Keith replied, "Yeah, I can build a car. We got some stuff and Dad said he'd build a motor." A short time later, Keith called Larry over to the shop and pointed at two frame rails on the floor. Larry said, "What's that?" and Keith told him, "That's our race car."

For the next year, Keith and the gang at the shop got into working on the little '27 T on custom rails. "I got off work at five and then started on that thing until 10, 11, 12, or one in the morning," Keith recalls. "We got the car out there and that itself was a huge undertaking." The first time out, things didn't work out so well in the motor department. The old flatheads had trouble digesting all that blown, injected alcohol. Just seeing the car run down the salt and function perfectly was enough; Vern and Ed Binggeli would eventually figure out the motor equation. Even though Keith is out of the car now, he is still proud that his dad and the crew took it out in 2002 and got a record with a 157-mile-per-hour two-way average for the yellow production Ford flathead V-8 engine/blown fuel modified roadster (XF/BFMR).

With so much behind him and so much ahead, Keith's eyes are focused on the future. "Hot rodding is my life," he says. "It's my dream to continue to build great cars in the traditional style. I have a lot of plans to educate people and carry on my family's tradition." Part of the plan is an invitational event Keith calls "The Hot Rod Revolution." The first one was held in Penngrove, California, in September 2006 and was a success that Keith hopes to repeat on a yearly basis.

As the late rain falls haphazardly on the roof of Rex Rods & Chassis, the sun sets. The stories stop and the lights go out on the busy shop. In the darkness, the cars hunker down and wait for morning when the work will recommence.

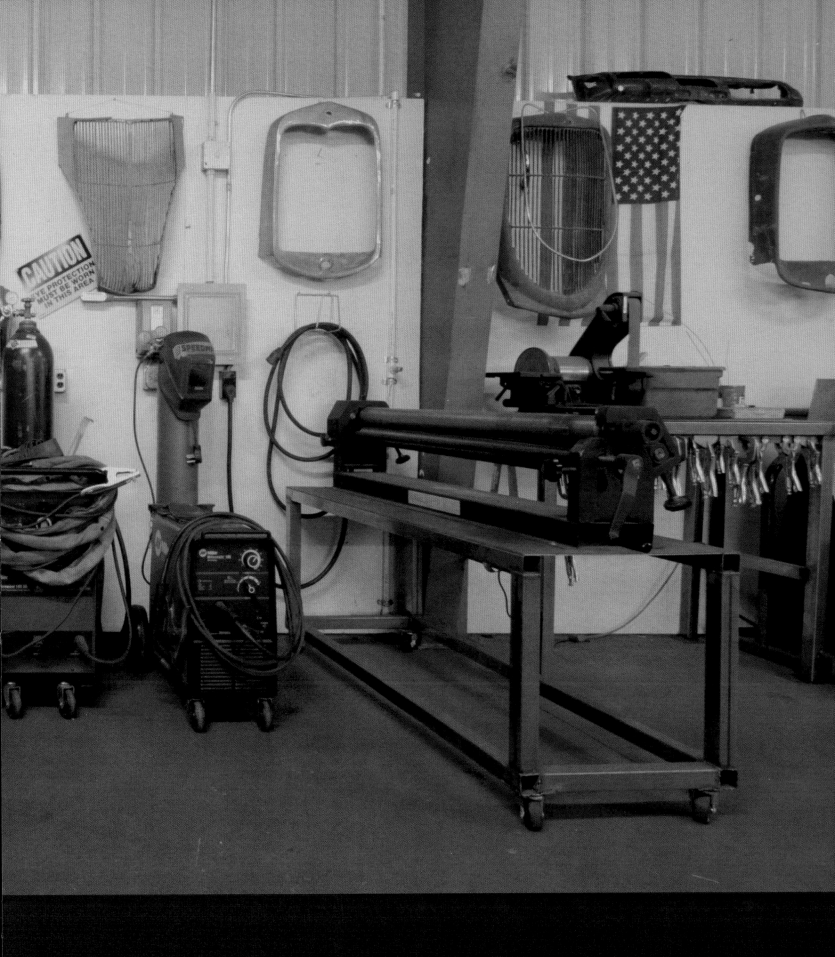

Rudy Rodriguez

Rudy's sons, Sonny (left) and Jasper (right).

THE HOUSE RUDY RODRIGUEZ BOUGHT BY SELLING NEARLY EVERYTHING HE OWNED SITS IN A LEAFY SUBURBAN SECTION OF ORANGE, CALIFORNIA.

There is little chance a casual passerby would ever guess that one of the United States' eminent hot rod builders lives in and works out of this house. No sign or website or flag-waving of any sort goes on here, and that is just how Rudy likes it. He is a bit of a recluse who values his time here on earth and intends to use it wisely. Ask anybody in the new generation of hot rodders and customizers who their influences or favorites might be, and Rudy's name invariably comes up. In a world where a good reputation is hard to come by, much less keep, Rudy is a true king, a real gentleman, and a full-time family man.

Rudy is wiry and intense; at first meeting he can seem laconic, his bullshit detector set on high. No time is spared for the tire kicker or social climber. Once deemed to be without false motives, you are given the gift of meeting a man with a truly big heart. The cadence of his speech rises and falls, speeds and slows, then pauses for emphasis with the rhythm of a natural storyteller. There is some pain in his voice—pain that comes from over 20 years of working nonstop on automobiles. At 19 years old, Rudy went to work as a mechanic on VWs and stayed for 20 years. The steady day job provided cash for a burgeoning hot rod habit that began with a yellow '34 Ford coupe.

Perhaps the meanest-looking chopped '33 Ford five-window coupe ever. The stance is high and dead nuts on the money. A single two-barrel sits on the bone-stock flathead.

The coupe was an all-original hot rod built in 1957 that Rudy purchased off a used car lot. Rudy resurrected the tired old coupe and put it on the road. "It was my daily driver for 10 years," Rudy says. "We took it on a run in '86 and people were like, 'Why do you have whitewalls on that car?' Back then, nobody had whitewalls. We took it to Paso Robles in '88 and '89 and it was still oddball! Both years I won first place in the hot rod class, but there was only two frickin' hot rods! The rest were customs." There might have been only two hot rods at those Paso meets, but the job Rudy did on the car and the way he set it up started to catch people's attention and the car grabbed a feature in *American Rodder*.

As Rudy delves further into his own story, he gets pensive, then backs up. He tells about building choppers and customs in 1984 with the help of his good friend Dominick, then quickly points out two men who put him on the right track when he began his 1951 Mercury. "When I chopped my Mercury, that was the first car I ever decided to cut," he explains. "A friend of mine, an older guy named Dale Evans, helped. He never chopped a car either, but he knows how to do metalwork. He was good. I go, 'You think we can chop this?' He goes, 'Hell yeah, we can chop it.' I go, 'You ever done it?' He says, 'Heck no!' I'm, 'How do you know we can do it?' He's, 'Because I KNOW we can!' So, between him and me, we chopped it. It came out fully righteous. He taught me the right way of doing it. He told me to keep my mouth shut and watch. And ever since then I've learned myself, doing all this crazy stuff and I've had lots of help. But I've always done it right because he *taught me* from the very beginning what's right. I'm *glad* somebody like him

Rudy's '51 Merc at a Viejitos car club picnic.
Rudy was president of the Orange County chapter.

Rudy's old street-fightin' '55 Chevrolet packin'
a blown small-block built by his friend, Brian Stairs.

taught me. The only thing about that job was that we had to listen to Jimmy Buffett. We worked on the Mercury for six months and every single night I had to listen to Jimmy Buffett."

Rudy laughs at the memory and continues, "And there's my friend Bill Holland. He has a shop called BRC. He's been in hot rods for years. He's the one who taught me all about building chassis. Anytime I needed anything, he'd come to my house and show me. Now it's bitchin' because I can help him with questions about the early hot rods that I know he doesn't know much about. No I'm stoked that I can *finally* help him."

The passion and emotion with which Rudy tells the story of how Bill and Dale helped him in his early years come through in his gestures and body language. It is also evident in his eyes. The things Rudy has been lucky to have all along have been his eyes and what they are capable of discerning. "The eye part you're born with," says Rudy. "I was lucky to have it." Rudy's eye for what is cool and what's not was evident from the start, but his eye for proportioning and detail and presentation really became apparent with his trendsetting "green truck." The ultralow and crazy proportioning totally worked, with a six-gun for a shifter and crazy *putas* adorning the sides for emphasis. When he took it to Paso in 2003, he had to register under an alias due to high jinks he pulled there back in '94. After the meet, the truck became influential, spawning a host of imitators. Magazines did features and some dubbed it "Rudy Style." To this day, a caller or two still gets through to Rudy and asks for one built "Rudy Style." Tough luck. "Rudy Style" is always on the move and the

A rear view of the '29 Model A roadster that will one day go to Rudy's son Jasper.

green truck is long gone, sold to a man whose taste proved too conservative to leave the *putas* and the slogan *buenas par tocar la corneta* emblazoned on the satin-green paint.

The truck won a trophy that Rudy didn't even bother picking up. Strange behavior for some, but not for this man who says, "It's nice to know you've made your reputation, not that someone made it for you." Another time, a car that Rudy built won a prestigious award but the plaque at the show gave Rudy no credit. Rudy shrugged his shoulders and let it go. His friends, however, weren't having it and they kicked the plaque over so many times that it was finally withdrawn. None of this bothers Rudy. He couldn't care less about fame. Although the plaque didn't give Rudy the credit, his kids saw him build the car. The kids know he built it and that is enough for Rudy. "It's for my kids. All that matters is that they know."

"There is something you guys need to know about Rudy," states Rudy's wife, Mia, over lunch. "Hot rods and all that take second place. Rudy is 100 percent Dad all the time." It shows in the way he lights up when he and Mia get to telling stories about his sons, Jasper and Sonny, who were born straight into a hot rod cradle.

Mia: "When Jasper was 15 months old, he took a pick hammer to the back of Rudy's '51 [Mercury]."

Rudy and his wife, Mia.

The yellow '34 Ford coupe as it appeared in *American Rodder*.

Rudy: "He used to watch me do metalwork. We were in the back yard with friends and all the sudden I heard it. It was like, bobong, bong, bong. We were like, 'What is that?' He took the pick, the pointy part of it, all over the back of the Merc. I had painted it black. It was done. The car was perfect. I had to repaint the trunk. He just ruined it, put dents all over it...I just had to laugh."

Mia: "When Jasper went to preschool, he handed the teacher the plastic play tools and he asked, 'Where are the real tools?'"

Rudy: "Yeah, he played with real tools for so long that when he went to school we had to explain to him that the plastic ones were cool too. And my boy, Sonny, if I throw something away, like a headlight switch or something, he'll pick the trash and hide it in his room. I ask him why he's saving this stuff and he'll shoot back, 'Why are you throwing it away?' I'll tell him 'cause it's broken and he just says, 'Why don't you fix it?' I don't even argue anymore. He's got all kinds of stuff in his room."

That the boys tie into the cars, there is no doubt. Rudy built his '29, patinaed 3x2bbl, small-block stroker-motored roadster with as much help as Jasper could give. The car will one day belong to Jasper and he knows it.

Rudy points out a fenderless, flathead-powered '33 Ford coupe with a genius and sinister chop that he's building. The windshield sports just over 6 inches of glass. Rudy says, "It's comin' out pretty good 'cause I been buying parts for it for the last five

years. I hope I don't have to sell it." Rudy tried to trade the coupe to Jasper for the roadster so that he could sell the roadster, but Jasper wasn't having it. Jasper told his dad, "You ain't selling my roadster, Daddy. That's my car."

Rudy says, "He made me feel like a jerk. He goes, 'Please don't sell my roadster, Daddy,' and when he said it I almost cried. I said, 'You know what? You're right.'" One day Jasper will be driving a 91-year-old car to school.

The younger boy, Sonny, is into bikes and Rudy has all the parts for him to one day build and ride a raked and stretched '53 panhead. Rudy says the boys do well in school and that's what's important. "Sonny can start building the bike when he's 12 or 13," Rudy says. "If he wants to ride a bike to school, then so be it."

Rudy hopes that one day the boys will want the business and he can give it to them. At the very least, he could use the help. Ask anyone who's worked as a mechanic for a living and they'll tell you about the physical toll it can exact. Rudy is pretty much a one-man show and a damn good one. On Paul Hoffman's '32 Ford Bonneville race car (see below), he did get help from expert metal man Tommy Leonardo Jr., who also is responsible for some of the paint. Rudy gives

The construction of this '29 Model A roadster is top-notch throughout. A stock '53 Mercury flathead with iron heads is topped by a polished Fenton intake with two Ford 94s. Rudy's personal '34 coupe is in the background. The pinched and bobbed frame is from the Kiwi Connection. Leather interior is by Carol Knapp.

credit to "The Kiwi" for some of the excellent frame rails he uses, but in the end it is all Rudy, all the time. He freely acknowledges the ups and downs of being a sole proprietor working at home. "When I had a screwed-up day at the VW shop, I used to drive home, couldn't wait to have a beer," he recalls. "I'd pull in and my wife and kids would come running out to hug me. Dude. They could make *any* nightmare day better. Now, when a day is wrong there is no going home 'cause you *are* home. The kids come home at three o'clock and we're stoked to see each other, but they know when it's a bad day. They hug me and go inside the house. They know already. That's the part that kinda sucks."

Despite whatever painful side effects he may feel, Rudy remains enthusiastic about his trade. His dedication shows in his detail work and savvy design features that never detract from the best lines the car originally had to offer. He is also passionate about speed and power. Racing is in his blood; he once crewed on an A/Gas coupe in black primer called *The Beatnik.* Rudy and his blown straight-axle '55 Chevy were no strangers to the drags or the street races either. These days it's more about the building—after all, there are bills to pay.

The super-badass former race car restored by Rudy for owner Paul Hoffman to its 1953 configuration with a full-race 296-ci 1946 Mercury flathead, Sharp heads, and a Baron-Tattersfield four pot with 97s set up by Jere Jobe. The Hallibrand quick-change rear end was set up by the Hotrod Works in Nampa, Idaho. Built in 1950 by Jack Quinton and Bob Joehnck, the car was a record holder at the lakes and at Bonneville. The fastest record it ever copped was at 154 miles per hour with a De Soto Hemi for power. The fastest speed it ever achieved was 178 miles per hour with a blown Olds.

Rudy's '29 Model A roadster.

Cowl detail on the sinister chopped '33.

Rudy and his '29 Model A roadster powered by a 383-ci stroker small-block Chevy.

Rudy's most recent car, and one that satisfies both urges, is a race-pedigreed '32 three-window Bonneville coupe. Unlike some of the "chitty chitty bang bang cars that do nothing" for him, this coupe is fast and has nine salt-flat records and a story. Mark Morton of *Hop Up* saw it and said it was the bitchin'est car Rudy ever built. Rudy and owner Paul Hoffman drove it over to original owner Jack Quinton's house. Jack was 94 years old at the time and when he saw the car, he cried. Soon enough he was back behind the wheel for a test drive through time.

Rudy kept the car true to form, and in the end it became an amalgamation of several of the car's previous incarnations. Salt had rotted the lower 8 to 12 inches of the car, and when Rudy got it chunks of NOS salt were still inside. Now, thanks to Rudy, Leonardo, and Hoffman, the car is not only beautiful but ready to rip, too. The interior is faithful; the original World War II bomber seat is the only place to sit. To keep you company, there is the fuel tank, shifter, and steering wheel. The inside door skins are punched aircraft-style by Tommy, and Rudy re-created the dinky original-style roll bar. The Rudy Rodriguez/Eric Hanson chassis is a beautiful example of form and function. From the rear, only the Halibrand quick change is visible because the transverse leaf is hung in front of it and friction shocks are employed. The frame is tied with a Swiss-cheese crossmember and everything underneath and inside is painted a dull silver to accent the "Blue Oval" blue body. With suicide doors, no headlights, and a mean lakes chop, the car is all business. The 296-ci flathead with four 97s puts an exclamation point on the whole deal. When you goose it, she jumps. Beware and be ready.

This car and the period '29 Model A roadster that Rudy just built and sold show that he is far from being finished. When his sinister '33 hits the streets, a whole new chapter of "Rudy Style" will commence. The road this one-man show travels may not always be paved with gold, but Rudy knows where he came from and where he is going. With his wife and kids at his side, the going is just that much smoother.

Mike Smith

California Hot Rods

UP IN THE SIERRA FOOTHILLS OF CALIFORNIA THERE IS A SMALL TOWN BY THE NAME OF SONORA.

At one time, gold brought people here; now, 150 years later, the gold has all but dried up. The hills are peaceful and laced with roads perfect for a drive in a hot rod, and up here on the edge of sleepy Sonora, there is a hub of activity known as California Hot Rods, run by a man named Mike Smith.

Long before Mike opened his shop, his father Leroy began indoctrinating him into the world of hot rods and fabrication. Leroy has been into rodding since 1958 and his knowledge runs deep. He's built and restored dozens of rods and still drives his Fiat Topolino on custom 2x3-inch rails wherever the road and the '62 Caddy motor will take him. Leroy has a straight-shooting, no-BS personality that he shares with Mike. He also taught Mike the basics of welding and everything that he knew about building cars.

In high school, Mike enrolled in a sort of work-release program that allowed him to spend most of his time off campus in the shop building hot rods. Mike bought a '27 T roadster (that he still owns today) and got down to work, harvesting ideas from

The Family Smith, left to right: Mitch, Robby, Kristi, and Mike.

The '35 Ford pickup was already chopped when it came into the shop but more is scheduled to come out. Under the channeled cab is a completely custom-built 2x4-inch rectangular-tube chassis built by Mike Smith to take the punishment of a blown small-block Chevrolet going through a Muncie four-speed to a Currie Ford 9-inch rear. The front view really shows off the 5-inch dropped Magnum axle.

old hot rod yearbooks. He got the inspiration for the perfectionist welds he's known for today when he ordered roadster parts from Pete & Jake's. "I got some Pete & Jake's parts and looked at the welds and they were perfect," Mike remembers. "Ever since then, I just tried to model after those [welds] and I just did it. I never took a class."

After high school, Mike kept building cars but held down a day job building coffee-packing machinery. In his home garage, after work and on weekends, Mike put in extra hours to build the cars. He did take a little time off to do some drag racing and build show-winning VWs. The Volks deal lasted almost 10 years, until hot rods once again reigned supreme. As his reputation grew, Mike discovered he was making more money after hours than he was by putting in a 40-hour week at his straight job. Once again, what started as a hobby grew into a way of life.

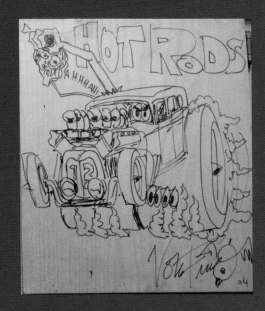

The first California Hot Rods shop opened in 2001 in a 1,700-square-foot space. Mike approached his new business with customary zeal and took on all comers. Hot rods were and still are the backbone, but everything else under the customized sun found its way into the shop. Mike likes a challenge and did it all, short of paint jobs. It wouldn't be incorrect to refer to Mike as a workaholic. In just one year, the business outgrew that first shop and moved to its present 3,500-square-foot location.

In case the hot rods parked out front aren't enough to clue you in to what's happening inside, a sign hangs on the front of the steel-clad shop. Your first impression upon walking through the roll-up is "holy shit." The doorman is Mike's old yellow '27 T roadster, in for a full makeover. On the right, a wall full of photos, model cars, posters, and automotive artwork steals your glance, but only for a second. The chassis table is dead ahead, and a mean-lookin' 1935 Ford pickup is taking shape. All sorts of steel tubing and frame members occupy the right-

Wall art by Von Franco.

The California Hot Rods nerve center.

hand wall. Almost everywhere, parts await their cue. Next to the pickup is a tough '59 Impala stuffed with motor and rubber getting a custom exhaust and suspension work. Two Chevy street rod pickups are also in, along with a crazy-as-hell '39 Mercury convertible that Leroy is working to completion. A '29 Ford Model A roadster rounds out the workload on this visit.

The space is organized well enough, so it doesn't feel crowded. If all the cool cars and machinery don't catch your eye, the walls—filled with eye candy—will. Leroy's area alone can keep you busy for an hour. He's got the coolest vintage go-karts hanging on the wall, along with airplanes and his own collection of cool. Throughout the shop there are antiques, vintage signage, and bric-a-brac galore. Sophia Loren oversees it all from the back wall over a shrine to auto-Americana. In the far corner and behind a wall there is drilling, milling, and cutting machinery. More spare parts hang from the walls, and roadster bodies are cooling out too. There's a bead blaster that can handle a bare block, a sheetmetal break, and an English wheel. Chisels, hammers, bags, dollies, you name it. Any tool is available, and if they don't happen to make the one Mike needs, he'll make it himself. Anything can be fabricated in this shop and done right. It's a matter of not only pride, but nature.

There is so much going on at once that you'd think you were at the North Pole the week before Christmas. Mike concentrates on bringing in the business, building chassis, and overseeing the workflow. His dad

This photo represents a fourth of the shop. Behind the rack with the Topolino body on top are more machine tools. Cars getting worked on in this shot include (left to right) a Ross Bava's 1930 Model A roadster, Todd Wiegel's 1959 Chevy pickup, and Wayne Dickerson's 1934 Ford pickup.

handles special projects, and when Mike's not looking, Leroy digs into his vintage go-karts. Cousin John Logsdon assembles, cuts, welds, hammers, and gets his kicks in his hot rod '36 Ford pickup. Dan Shimer packs his burly frame under any and all dashes to wire the rides so the lights burn as bright as the nitrous shots. Ryan Hamilton takes care of parts procurement and Mike's wife, Kristi, balances the books and keeps the ball on the ground. It's full time and Mike and Kristi also have two boys, Robby (six years) and Mitch (four years). You want to talk about comin' and goin'? Talk to Mr. and Mrs. Smith.

Under the skin is where a California Hot Rod–built car really shines. The chassis are built to race car standards. The perfectionist welds not only look good, but are strong as well. "I go overboard on chassis," Mike states. "Nothing will break there." One chassis Mike built was involved in a pretty serious wreck. The tubing tore apart, but the welds didn't and the frame stayed straight. Today, it lives on in a new coupe. An onlooker at a car show was checking out one of Mike's rides in its under-construction state and tried to get under Mike's skin about all the tubing in the chassis. The guy poked around and finally asked, "Why so much tubing? Doncha think it's too much?" Mike replied, "No, it's just enough. You take all the weight out of one of these cars and most people forget to put some back in." Mike's account of his own work makes perfect sense when you take into account that the car in question was already packing some heavily blown cubes.

Not all the cars built by California Hot Rods are slated for such heavy horsepower, and the more traditional rides reflect that fact in their chassis. The '32 Fordor that Kristi bought Mike for his thirty-second birthday is a case in point. Mike pinched and step-boxed the rails, laid in a Vern Tardel K-member, and did some custom tying up but stopped just short of all-out. The Fordor is more of a traditional piece with flathead power, a dropped front axle, "big C-notches" in the rear, and a mono leaf in the front and buggy springs out back. The body is in as-is condition—straight, patinaed, and just

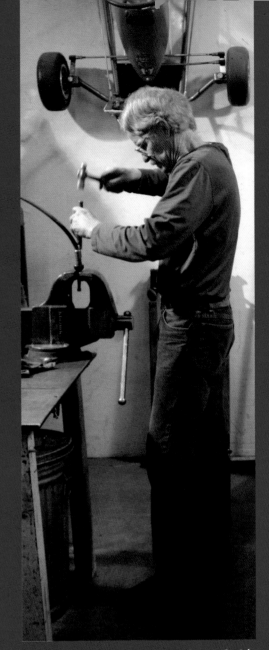

Leroy Smith

Leroy Smith's Fiat Topolino. This car is a rebuild of a car Leroy once owned back in the '60s.

The 1925 Model T that Mike Smith's had since he was a teenager. In this incarnation, a blown mouse with Dart heads sits between the rails.

Mike Smith

right. Mike says, "It would've been nice to finish it, but it got so much ink the way it is that I don't wanna mess it up. Besides, finished cars are a pain in the ass. I've got kids and bicycles and I don't want to worry about it when it's in the garage."

Just because it doesn't have paint, don't go calling it a rat rod. The level of craft in the Fordor and all of Mike's cars preclude such a moniker, and Mike isn't afraid to let a little venom loose on the rat rod phenomenon: "I don't fit the whole scene. It started out kind of cool, but then they started building these jokers. Some people think the biggest, rustiest piece of shit they can bolt together is cool because they can get the most attention with it."

There is no signature car from California Hot Rods—they all share Mike's obsession to detail. Any and all gussets are gracefully curved and drilled. Front shock mounts intelligently meld into headlight brackets. Headers and exhaust systems are done in-house too. Even a mundane item like an exhaust hanger is treated like a center-stage item. Each one includes a gentle radius that matches the OD of the pipe to which it is welded. "The only person that's gonna notice it is the person you run over," cracks Mike.

His latest craze is smoothie radiator plumbing crafted from up to 10 to 15 individual pieces of tubing. Mike says, "I get into a zone, especially when I'm

on the chassis table. I'm always trying to better myself. Const[...] working on fit and finish, trying to make my welds better. I get [...] my own little world and trip out and build things. When you [...] right down to it, I just like building hot rods."

Mike is also a firm believer in keeping a car true to an era or s[...] His '32 sedan is a case in point, with its step-boxed frame, [...] Tardel K-member, and flathead power. His roadster is somew[...] "within '62 to '65, and that's where it's gonna stay." This min[...] keeps the cars from becoming a hodgepodge of ill-conce[...] ideas and also allows for a little leeway in the build.

For inspiration, Mike turns to books and race cars. He also [...] his friend Jimmy White's cars and the cars out of Roy Brizio's s[...] "I do a lot of modeling after Roy's stuff," Mike says. "And I [...] look at Cole [Foster]'s work and [Jimmy] Shine's. I love lookir[...] their stuff." Pete Chapouris and Jim Jacobs come up again, [...] "My two hot rod idols would be Pete and Jake. The way they [...] things is just bitchin'. The stances on their cars have been d[...] on from day one. Anytime I ever saw a picture of one of their [...] I'd cut it out and study it."

Hot rod TV shows play a role, too, but not for what you'd thir[...] just watch 'em so I can see something in the background. T[...] how I got some ideas for my chassis jig. I was watching [...] [Coddington]'s show and hit rewind and paused it and act[...] sketched it out on a piece of paper." Mike laughs and adds, "I [...] have fun watching those guys pull their hair out 'cause I can s[...] the couch and have beer and relax."

For Mike, pen and paper play no role in the visualizing and b[...] ing of cars. He explains, "I don't draw, I don't sketch, I don[...]

Right: Mike's cousin and coworker, John Logsdon.

Bottom: Johnny's '36 Ford at speed on the old Highway 49. As low as this truck is, the stout and well-thought-out chassis and suspension keep a smile on your face and the oil pan intact.

IT'S NOT A FUCKING *Rat Rod*, IT'S JUST NOT FINISHED!

anything. I picture the car in my head and I know exactly what the car is gonna look like." When it came time to chop cousin John Logsdon's '36 pickup cab, Mike looked at it, went to work, and took 6 inches out of the roof. When they set the roof back down, it fit nearly perfectly. Mike has the aesthetic and engineering eye for sure.

What really puts California Hot Rods up there with the best, though, is the sheer scope of the operation and the amount of dedication it takes to make it run. No job is too large or too small; Mike's not "afraid of any of it." To build one high-quality hot rod is no small endeavor, but to have four going at once is sheer madness. To keep the quality high and the customer satisfied are equally demanding. You can put in a ten-hour day and only six will show on the timecard—any mistakes are on your own time and Mike believes that is in true fairness to the customers, who get exactly what they pay for. He explains, "I don't go after store-bought anything. I don't mass-produce a chassis. We build one-off hot rods. They're not kit cars. You can look at one of our cars and say, 'This didn't roll out of an assembly line hot rod shop.'"

In the end, it is sweat that runs the business. "I bust my ass for it," says Mike. "I have a wife and two kids and a house payment. I get up at 6 a.m. and don't go to bed until 10 o'clock. A lot of times, I'll stay at the shop and won't get out of there until 7. I like to dick around, so I need the money to be able to dick around eventually. I don't wanna do this forever. I want to have a garage with some bitchin' shit in it and build a car when I want to. If the boys want to take over the business, that'd be great. I'll go work for them. I'll fart around with my go-kart." For the would-be builder, Mike has this advice: "You have to constantly improve. Build, watch everything, and just learn. Don't think you're there...*ever.*"

From the looks of things, Mike heeds his own advice and riding around in a California Hot Rods ride is the proof. Early spring days in the Sierra Foothills are especially nice 2 inches off the highway at a stable 70 miles an hour in Logsdon's '36. A ride down old State Route 49 in Mike's Fordor with the flathead purring and Leroy's Topolino in the rearview on the way to the roadhouse to quaff a few is truly food for hot rod thought...it's downright inspirational. Like Mike says, "Watch everything and learn."

This '32 Fordor is the present Mike received from his wife, Kristi, on his 32nd birthday. Since acquiring the car Mike has put in custom crossmembers to connect American Stamping rails, and a vintage 5-inch dropped axle. A Tardel K-member cradles the Ford flathead stuffed with a Mercury crank, Jahn's pistons, and a Winfield cam. Headers are custom by Mike, and the wheels are 16-inch Ford wires.

Jimmy White

Circle City Hot Rods

Circle City *HOT RODS*

WELDING & FABRICATION

HEADING SOUTH FROM LOS ANGELES, THE 5 FREEWAY CRAWLS THOUGH A NEVER-ENDING URBAN LANDSCAPE.

Where one town begins and another ends, a simple sign suffices to let the traveler know that there are lines drawn under the cement. It is hard to imagine that acres of orange groves once spread across the flatlands to the sea. Here, in Orange, California, is where Jimmy White grew up and chose to stay.

Like many young Americans, Jimmy's interest in cars began in high school. A 1965 fastback Mustang got the juices flowing. By the time Jimmy turned 16, he had built and installed his first motor and was on the streets. Now established as a car guy, Jimmy recalls that his "old friends didn't hang out with me anymore. I hung out with a couple of rockabillies, some heshers, and the punkers." Music began to play a role in shaping Jimmy's aesthetic, and he was listening to and attending the concerts of Big Sandy, Russell Scott, The Paladins, and The Blasters. He began to hang out at the legendary hole-in-the-wall called The Doll Hut. Jimmy says, "For me, discovering all this stuff was like finding an old friend."

This Southern California rockabilly scene "evolved into hot rods. Some guys had '50s cars, but guys like the Shifters spun it off and were like, let's build a traditional hot rod." Jimmy also recalls seeing Jimmy Shine driving a Model A to high school in the '80s when it seemed like nobody was driving hot rods anymore. Citing Rudy Rodriguez's yellow rod, Shines' Model A, Kevin "Sinus" Sledge's '28 T, and the music as influences, Jimmy White was inspired to try his hand at a traditionally flavored hot rod. It was no longer enough to drive around any old car.

In 1996, Jimmy purchased a 1931 Model A, five-window coupe as a roller with a 331-ci Hemi and a three-speed. At the time, by his own admission, Jimmy did not know how to weld or "even read a tape measure." To no avail, his father discouraged his son's newfound passion. Jimmy was dead set on building his ride and went about learning to weld. When he eventually got the car on the street, some of the reactions weren't what he expected. "I'd take it to work and my boss was

A 1931 Model A coupe body with headers and final assembly by Circle City Hot Rods. An 8BA flathead lives behind the '32 grille shell.

like, 'Man, you're gonna get killed in this thing. You gotta make it safer.' So, I'm all, 'I don't wanna scary car. I don't wanna die in my car. I gotta learn how to do this.' And once I got involved, I applied myself 110 percent. I went to school to learn how to TIG weld. I just tried really, really hard."

Having set his course, Jimmy got a job with Rod Millen building rally and off-road race cars and trucks. Working with the skilled fabricators and engineers at the shop helped Jimmy to refine his welding skills and also taught him the value in seeing a project as an integrated sum of its individual parts. Jimmy also learned the hows and whys of building a strong and durable chassis. This led to a job fabricating chassis for Boyd Coddington from 2000 to 2002.

On the side, in the garage at home, Jimmy was helping his friends and his friends build and work on their rides. His collection of parts began to grow and so did his skills. Opening a shop and going into business on his own was the next big step. When the time came, Jimmy approached opening "Circle City Hot Rods" with the same dogged determination that sent him from being a rat rodder who couldn't even weld to the accomplished crafts-man that he is today.

Circle City opened in 2002. Its present locale is in a nondescript industrial park, the sort of setting that exists on the fringes of every American city to serve the needs of small businesses. One half of the shop is devoted to storage, and the other is for the day-to-day tasks of building high-quality hot rods from the ground up. The shop is busy and looks the part. Welders, a milling machine, a lathe, drill presses, sheet metal breaks, shears, and rollers permit virtually any part to be fabricated in-house, and most parts are indeed done in-house. The walls are filled with tools and posters. Music is constantly in play, anything from Skynrd to an ironic (or maybe not so ironic) penchant for Elton John.

When Jimmy isn't bent to working, he's on the phone dealing with customers. Fernando "Ferny" Alonso comes by on Wednesdays to help out and work on his own '31 Model A. Ferny is also responsible for the solid engines powering several of the Circle City rides. Flatheads, small-blocks, Fire Domes, and the beautiful 324-ci Olds in

This '32 Brookville-bodied roadster shows off Circle City's abilities and aesthetic. Fernando Alonso built the punchy 324 Olds motor topped with two Stromberg Aerotypes on an Edmunds manifold. The Kiwi Connection rails are tied in the best Circle City tradition, and a T-5 chooses the ratios to send to the final 4.11:1 ratio in the Ford 9-inch rear. Charlie Hutton and Andrew Patterson each get credit for the body and paint.

Jimmy's '32 roadster showcase Ferny's machining and assembly skills. The whiplash performance the engines are capable of pay open-pipe tribute to the sharp tuning skills Fernando learned from his father.

Jimmy calls the aesthetic and design shots at Circle City and will build whatever it takes to get the job done right, right on down to the headers and exhaust systems. Each header set is unique for every ride he builds, and they are strong and well fit. Chassis work is Jimmy's real forté and it really shows when you get down and dirty, and roll under one of his rides. The frame rails are boxed and tied fore, aft, and amidships with tubular crossmembers that are every bit as elegant as they are strong. When the application dictates, the crossmembers are gusseted as well.

By his own admission, Jimmy tends to overbuild a bit, but everything is functional and gives the impression of strength, durability, and roadworthiness. Shock brackets, motor mounts, and trans mounts get the "treatment" as well. Where a square or rectangle might suffice, a gentle arc is cut into or onto the piece. On top of the frame rails, which frequently come from The Kiwi Connection, Jimmy bolts a square-tube subfloor for extra strength and then lays down the floor skin and bolts on the body.

If you can't get up close and personal by rolling under one of the Circle City–built cars, you are never gonna see all this work. That's too bad, but when you drive one of these cars you'll know it's all in there from

The beautifully detailed Alonso-built Olds in Jimmy's '32 roadster.

Popeye and Bluto

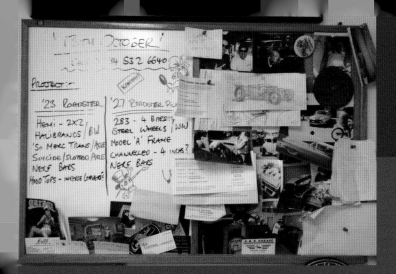

the solid, responsive, and predictable ride characteristics. Jimmy knows full well that most people will never see the elegant brackets and gussets he creates, and it does not bother him at all. He truly enjoys the work. Besides, he knows what is in each and every car he builds, even if you don't.

With business just getting heavier, Jimmy and the crew have less time for the finessing of sheet metal. This task now falls to master metal man Jesus Salas, whose work can be seen on many top builders' rides. To really understand Jesus' skills, you have to step in and see a car in the middle of the process. The result of his labor is sweet hammer and dolly work, with a skim of lead that's ready for paint. The way he can move and shape metal, you'd think he was working with Play-Doh.

In paint or in primer, the finished cars out of Circle City are beautiful and durable examples of traditional hot rods meant to be driven. In the interest of driving and power-handling, a T-5 trans or Muncie four-speed sends the torque from the Alonso-built motors to a Ford 9-inch. It goes a bit against the grain of the purist's "traditional" hot rod, but once you've had a ride you'll forget all about that action and know why Jimmy says "hot rods make people happy." You'd have to have a heart of coal and a wooden soul to not be wearing a shit-eating grin after taking a spin.

All this fancy welding and ride quality doesn't add up to a hill of rusted brake drums if you don't have "the eye." One of the hot rod builder's most valuable tools is the set of eyes he was born with. "I look at proportion more than anything," Jimmy explains. "I'll experiment with it too. As I'm mocking the car

: Cars in the Circle City Shop include (front to rear) a flathead-powered roadster, Model A Hemi roadster, and Paul Bormann's Hemi-powered pickup.

The lowered Gary Howard–inspired '57 Cadillac Jimmy built for his wife, Michelle, pictured in a near-perfect setting.

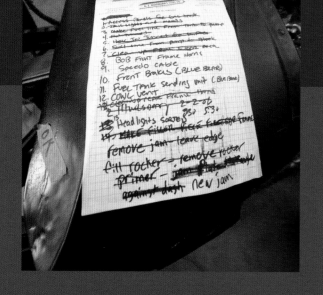

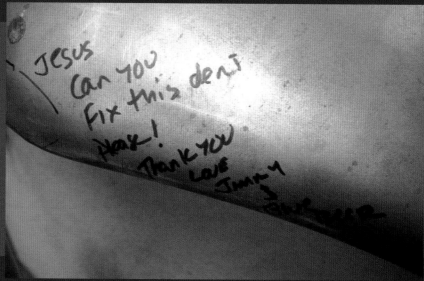

up, we'll raise or lower the engine; we'll change the stance and the ride height. I'll keep the wheelbase tight and get the engine up close to the radiator. I don't like dead space and I like the engine prominent. In my eyes, it's all about the engine. I'll just sit and stare at things sometimes to figure something out and, sometimes, just watching TV, it'll come to me." That's hot rods on the brain all the time and the payoff comes in the form of well-crafted rides that eschew gee-gaw adornment and overtly cartoonish proportions.

For inspiration, Jimmy says he "looks to the past and I look at some of the cars people are building now. I also think about race car style as inspiration." All the best hot rods have a little race car in them and Circle City's rods are no exception. A true purpose-built racer has yet to come out of the shop, but Jimmy has been looking out the corner of his eye and seeing salt. An A/Fuel roadster is going to be in the works, and Jimmy says, "I'd rather be building race cars than hot rods; it's easier because it's more function than style."

On the subject of today's trend toward traditional-looking-yet-rough hot rods, Jimmy pulls no punches. "Hot rodding is getting a bad name again because you see a lot of these cars and it looks like the guy just pulled it out of a riverbed," he says. "I don't know how well they're built. From the looks of things, they're pretty shaky. The thing is, cars weren't built like that in the '50s; they were built pretty well and the primer was just a step on the way to painting." When asked which builders he admires today, he mentions the Kennedy Brothers, Rudy Rodriguez, Mike Smith, and Cole Foster. He makes these pronouncements without cockiness and readily acknowledges the help he's received from his friends and his wife, Michelle. He knows where he is with himself and with his work, and it shows in the way he handles himself with his employees, his customers, and his friends. In short, Jimmy White is the real deal and Circle City Hot Rods is a heckuva machine.

Gary Howard

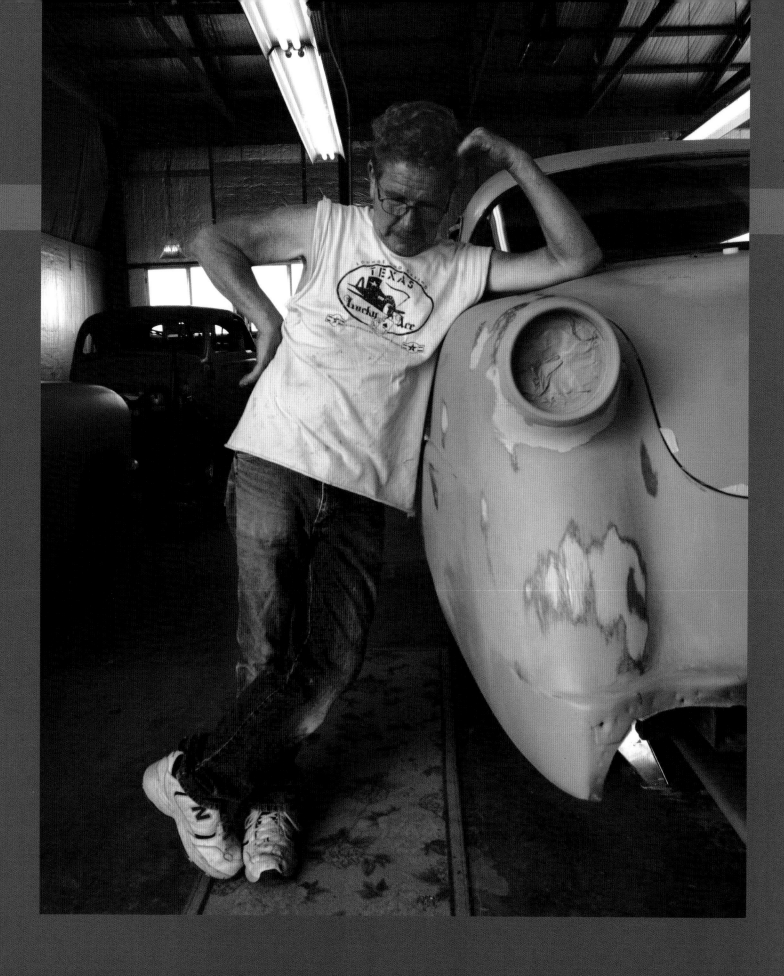

Some brush sketches from Gary's "Border Lord" era.

COLOR IS THE WORLD GARY HOWARD INHABITS.

His custom automotive paint and bodywork is the definitive study in understatement and depth. Applying years of experience to his techniques, Gary can create an entire world in a monochromatic quarter panel. Underneath the coats of clear, something is happening. Gentle pearls and mini flake conspire with the sun to create a chameleon-like effect that sometimes betrays, emphasizes, or disguises the true color. Once, there were vinyl LPs that looked black until you held them to the light; then they revealed themselves to be deep red or blue. A Gary Howard paint job can be like that. It can also assert itself with conviction.

On a Gary Howard–built custom, the body lines are crisp yet seem to melt into color. There are myriad body modifications that take enormous amounts of time and talent to execute. Sail panels, entire backlights, hoods, trunks, and grilles are changed. Abiding by tradition, door handles are removed, as is exterior trim deemed inessential to the car's design. Tops are ever-so-slightly chopped, to the point that even a trained observer might remain in disbelief. The layman might take the car for basically unmodified; he just knows it looks absolutely bitchin'. This is because the original design is held fast, but at the same time radically, yet subtly, changed. Gary divines the car's true character. When your car has been built and painted by Gary Howard, the one and only question is "How did he do it?"

Gary can do what he does because he has a foundation of knowledge as rich as his paint jobs, and a work ethic that allows him to do only his best work. He is a body man by trade and can

Gary back in the day in Council Bluffs, Iowa, posing on Papa's 1930 Chevrolet.

rightly be called a journeyman. Gary was raised on a farm out by Council Bluffs, Iowa. He says he "got into this whole thing by watching my dad mess around with old cars." He has fond memories of a '51 Mercury coupe with dual exhausts that his dad drove around in. For an eighth-grade art project, Gary meticulously drew his favorite cars, and if further proof of his early passion is needed, the very car in which he took his driver's license test recently resurfaced with Gary's teenage pinstripe job still on the valve covers. Gary remembers, "Cars were about the only thing I've ever done since high school. I did customs for fun, for myself really."

Fresh out of high school, Gary went straight to the body shop. For years, he made his living doing collision work and learned all aspects of the trade, from metal fabrication to prep and paint. During the '70s, he tried his hand at airbrush-style art for van murals, signing himself as "Border Lord" after the Kris Kristofferson song. By his own admission, Gary "can't draw worth a damn," so it was back to building, bodywork, and painting. Eventually his creative side won out and realized its outlet in customs. There would be no more soulless collision work for Gary Howard.

One thing that enabled Gary to go full-time was his new association with Jimmie Vaughan. When the two first met, Gary had no idea who Jimmie was. They met again at an auction where Jimmie was looking at the cars for styling cues, "parts and pieces," as Gary tells it. They struck up a conversation and realized they were both speaking the same aesthetic language. Jimmie asked Gary, "You work on cars for other guys, doncha? You wanna look at one of mine?" They drove up to Jimmie's house to look at a '51 Chevy that was in bad shape.

Gary tells it like this: "[Jimmie] didn't realize just how bad it was at the time, although I know he suspected it. We went to his house and looked at it, and two weeks later began our long-standing

Views of Mike Young's Howard-built '60 Impala show the elegant chop and drastically reworked tail panel with custom taillights. Custom-mixed abalone flake laid down by Gary is accented by scallops and flames by Rod Powell. Interior by master stitchman Vernon McKeane.

These views give some clues to the immediate surroundings and interior of the Howard shop. The car in bare metal in the upper right is a '39 five-window Ford getting a drastic rescue effort. The '54 Ford Victoria in primer at lower left is another Jimmie Vaughan–commissioned project.

The '52 Ford that Gary sold and then repurchased more than 10 years later. The red oxide is a cover-up for a particularly nasty shade of green the last owner put on the car.

friendship. I was still working at a local shop full-time, so the work on this car was done after hours in my garage. Many nights I would start work at 10:00 p.m., after everyone went to bed, and work until 2:00 a.m. Near the end of the project, I was spending so much time at home working on the '51 that I just didn't have time to go to work at the regular job. That was when I decided to do this full-time. I committed. I just said, 'That's it. I'm not doing anything else. No jobs. Nothing else. I'm committed to this thing one way or the other.'"

The '51 came to be known as *Violet Vision* after the color Gary custom-mixed. Gary reworked everything from the wheel openings to the hood corners, from the front to the rear. He was just giving a taste of his understated, clean-yet-radical work. In his own words, "This was the car that started it all." The custom world took note and *Violet Vision* snagged the cover of *Rod & Custom* in February 1991.

The fast friends became a collaborative, creative force to be reckoned with. Jimmie often dreams up the concepts and then they riff off the idea until they reach an understanding. Jimmie has a good eye and feel, but according to Gary, is "not bound by knowing anything about the process. When he says, 'Let's do this,' he doesn't know if he's talking about two hours or two weeks...but he's learning. He just knows what he thinks can happen." Fortunately for Jimmie, he's got a friend like Gary to make it happen, in steel and lead.

The '51 was the first of three cars to be "who knows how many" projects for this creative partnership. Jimmie commissioned Gary to do a '63 Riviera that Gary completed in 1992. Unbeknownst to Gary, Jimmie had some background info on a GM styling studio exercise. In the drawing a mild chop was involved, as was a new grille design; the car was supposed to be a new LaSalle, but Cadillac had no interest in the project and it became the '63 Buick Riviera. Ultimately, this was the inspiration for the incredible '63 Riviera Gary built for Jimmie. It features a 1 1/2-inch chop, a fully custom grille with '67 Chrysler headlights, and '59 Cadillac bullets. The car wears a resplendent coat of candy lime gold pearl with mini flake in the clear over a silver basecoat. This car, more than any other Gary has built, seems to inspire a bit of fear in fellow drivers on the street. A testament to the tasteful, well-executed body modifications and flawless paint came in the form of a Harry Bradley trophy. Howard and Vaughan's vision, craft, and reputation took another step forward.

The next car to roll out the door of the shop for Jimmie Vaughan was a '61 Cadillac Coupe DeVille, the first in a series of true wolves-in-sheeps'-clothing customs Gary has done. The Cad is ultraclean in emerald pearl, and takes what could pass for a mild custom into the world of the truly radical. Lee Pratt had already extended the deck lid and fabbed the dash and tach/speedo bracket when Gary got to it. He went to work and chopped the top just over an inch. Then he grafted in a third of the roof and entire rear window from a Cadillac six-window sedan. The fit and finish is perfect, and for all the world looks like it could be factory. The squaring off of the rear of the roof accentuates the round-to-angular, front-to-back Space Age lines of the original design. The car rides on '53 Buick wire rims and whitewalls, but closer examination reveals cheater slicks under the fender skirts. Those slicks come in handy with 500 inches of Caddy under the hood. The engine was originally supercharged, but now breathes through a single four-barrel on an Edelbrock intake.

Steve Wertheimer's '57 Caddy, nosed, decked, and painted in "lavendar mist" by Gary.

Word spread about Gary, and while he worked on Jimmie's cars he was commissioned by Mike Young to build a few more while he was at it. These projects began with a radical abalone-flaked 1960 Impala, which also happens to be the recipient of a Bradley award. Scallops and flames by Rod Powell accent the iridescent paint. At first, Gary was against both ideas but he says, "I had to admit I was wrong. The car needed them." The '60 Impala is also masterfully chopped just over an inch and the trailing curve of the roofline was changed to give it grace. It's all steel and the drastically reworked, perfect stainless trim does not lie.

An extremely mild 1960 Cadillac Coupe DeVille and a 1936 Ford three-window were the next projects Gary executed for Mike Young. The Caddy features the standard custom tricks like nosing, decking, and shaving. One lonesome stainless spear is left to break the monotony of the massive fuselage-shaped body. The body and paintwork are flawless. The paint is tricky, and won't reveal its true deep red color until the sun hits it just right. The top is done in a contrasting rainbow-and-abalone flake over silver. The little Ford coupe is nearly dead stock, with a few tricks like moving the spare cover down 2 inches to clean up the lines. Both of these cars exemplify just how something special can be done without drastic mods.

Gary enthusiastically explains modifications to the sail panel on Jimmie Vaughan's '63 Riviera. This car is also chopped just over an inch.

At the other end of the spectrum is a '49 Mercury four-door that Gary built for Dan Richards. Others have worked on the car, notably Roach's shop, which installed the Bowtie 502-ci motor and handled the trick fuel filler that resides behind one of the stock '49 taillights. The body and all of its modifications were done by Gary, and it was a five-year deal. Hood corners are rounded and the bumpers were made from multiple sections to get the right look. The inner fender skirts were reworked for a cleaner engine bay. Dan says he wanted a four-door "because I have little kids who ride in the back. It's a real 'Ward Cleaver' car." This is true except for that monster motor and the massive rubber out back, hidden by the flush-mounted '51 skirts. The paint is another example of a pearl over black, which only reveals the midnight blue hue when the sun strikes it.

All of this work comes from a friendly and unassuming man who is quick to laugh and gracious with guests. The shop is out in the middle of a field in Weir, Texas, about 20 miles or so from Austin. The shop was originally an extended two-car garage next to the trailer, which provides living quarters for Gary and his wife, Jo Ann. A few years ago, a larger steel building went up to provide the space needed for the volume of work that Gary now has.

On a hot, cloudless day in June, a gentle breeze stirs the heat and sets the tall grasses on the edge of the property to swaying. The heat shimmers and liquefies the color reflecting from cars resting all around the property. Some are in the middle of the mown grass and take on the appearance of

Jimmie's '63 showing off the custom grille with '67 Chrysler headlights, '58 Caddy bullets, and extended fender peaks. Another mild mod is the dummy brake cooling vents on the rear quarter panel that are now truly inset. The car rolls on Buick wires and the interior is another Vernon McKeane job.

Cut steering wheel on Gary's '52 Ford.

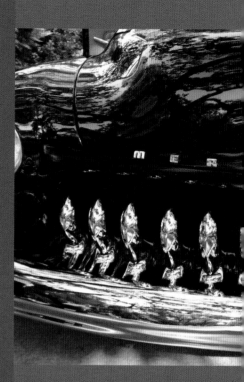

steel shrubbery. It's a bit lonely out here, and the only sound is the whir of a passing car or truck out on the ranch road. At the edge of the property, two trees give precious shade and grow through a collection of bodies peacefully surrendering their iron back to the earth one molecule and one flake at a time.

The whole scene is rather pastoral and Gary admits he finds comfort in the tableau. He explains, "I want to be out here, even if it's nothing else but sittin' on a tailgate and lookin' at all of it. It's insane, but I love it." The cars around the property serve as a palette and sort of an idea farm. If Gary is ever stuck on something, he can just walk around out here and get fresh inspiration or a part that will finish the job.

For Gary, each job is unique and he likens the task to constructing songs or organizing a band. The relationship Gary has with Jimmie Vaughan can be easily related to that of a songwriter and an arranger. All the parts and pieces must contribute to the good of the whole, and behind the scenes is where all the nuts and bolts of getting the finished product out to the audience, public, or buyer takes place. Gary is a collaborator and he likes to have input on all aspects of the project, from the motivation to the interior. In other words, "it's never just a paint job." Despite the apparent complexity of many of his creations, Gary never draws or sketches and never really measures too much. It's all in his eyes and in his hands. He is also a firm believer that the best customs are the understated ones, and his work is testimony to that.

Gary puts so much of himself into the cars that he feels like they are all his, even though other people own them. It is hard work

Above: This is Mike Young's extra-mild (and extra-cool) '60 Cadillac Coupe De Ville. This car exhibits the "less is more" approach with its beautiful paint and shave.

Middle: The grille and sectioned bumper on Dan Richard's '49 Mercury four-door.

and Gary does what he does on his own. He acknowledges that there is a downside to working alone, mainly that "there is only so much you can do." Nonetheless, he has done a tremendous amount of work in a short time and has begun to receive more and more recognition for it. Steve Coonan of *The Rodder's Journal* ran a "Custom Retrospective" in the 10th-anniversary issue and featured 3 of Gary's cars out of a total of 13 selected for the article. The recognition does not faze Gary or inflate his ego. "If no one ever saw this paint, I'd still be happy," he says. "[Recognition] doesn't drive me. It adds to it, though; but it's not why I do it. I enjoy this; if I had all the money in the world, I'd still be out here doin' this."

The fact is, all fans of customs and hot rods are lucky Gary Howard is building cars the way he is. They are examples of how to do 'em the right way. Gary explains how "I never really thought about it like that, but I kinda see it that way now. It just has to be done right and it has to look right. You gotta take the car and change it and make it look better. That's always been the challenge.

"The only regret I have is not figuring out 20 years earlier in my life why I was never satisfied with what I was doing day to day," Gary continues. "I shoulda been doing this. I hate to admit I'm having this much fun and only been doing it for 20 years." Judging from the fact that there are five projects going on at once in Gary's shop, the custom madness will not end anytime soon.

On the bags and in the weeds is Jimmie Vaughan's '61 Cadillac Coupe De Ville. Lucas headlights live under the extended brows.

Top: The absence of trim or door handles really makes the lines of the '61 Cadillac pop out of its emerald paint. The real kicker is the rear pillar and backlight grafted in from a "six window" sedan to go along with the mild chop.

Middle: Fit and finish are perfect. Here you get a glimpse of the reworked and barely extended deck lid done by Lee Pratt.

Bottom: Lee Pratt also gets credit for the cool dash on the '61. Interior by Craig Willits of Craig's Interior Design in Rockwall, Texas.

Acknowledgments

Michael Blanchard

Susan Foster

Billy F Gibbons

Patricia Hewett

Paul Hoffman

Jo Ann Howard

Suzi Hutsell

Jim Jard

Emily Ethel M.D. Johnson

Mike LaVella

Dennis Pernu

Dan Richards

Mia Rodriguez and family

Kristi Smith and family

Mary Tardel

Jimmie Vaughan and family

Steve Wertheimer

Michelle White

Mike Young and family

And, of course, all of the builders
featured and mentioned for allowing
us into their shops and garages.

Useful Web Links

California Hot Rods www.californiahotrods.com

Circle City Hot Rods www.circlecityhotrods.com

Gary Howard www.garyhowardcustoms.com

Rex Rod & Chassis www.rexrods.com

Salinas Boys www.salinasboys.com

South Austin Speed Shop www.southaustinspeedshop.com

DAVID PERRY, PHOTOS

David Perry has been burning film since he was 10 years old. Born in Denver, Colorado, and raised in Southern California, he studied photography at Art Center College of Design. A professional photographer since 1986, Mr. Perry has had his work published, collected, and exhibited across the United States and, indeed, worldwide. Current and past examples can be seen at www.davidperrystudio.com. His commercial clients include Corvette, Toyota, Polaris, Apple Computer, and the Las Vegas Convention and Visitors Authority.

Mr. Perry's other books include *Hot Rod* (Chronicle Books, 1997) and *Bordertown* (Chronicle Books, 1998), both with writer Barry Gifford, as well as *Hot Rod Pin-ups* (Motorbooks, 2005) and *Billy F Gibbons, Rock + Roll Gearhead* (MBI, 2005), the latter with Mr. Gibbons and Tom "TV" Vickers. Mr. Perry currently resides in Vallejo, California, and has one son, August. In 1999 he helped resurrect the Swanx car club (est. 1956).

KEVIN THOMSON, WORDS

Born in Binghamton, New York, and raised on eastern Long Island, Kevin Thomson migrated to Austin, Texas, to attend the University of Texas theater program. Punk rock and skateboard culture rendered university irrelevant and Mr. Thomson embarked on a zigzagging musical career. To date he has released seven LPs, two EPs, and several singles under the monikers Nice Strong Arm, Timco, Morning Champ, Touched By A Janitor, and most recently, Enablers.

Between long rides in smelly tour vans, Mr. Thomson kept alive a small flame for his love of writing and fast cars. In 1994, punk rock gadfly and Gearhead magazine publisher Mike LaVella offered him a regular column entitled "Bobo Tech" and Mr. Thomson began to pick up the pen and paper with regularity. Since then he has also contributed to Garage and Rust magazines, and has written essays for the Motorbooks titles *Hot Rod: The Photography of Peter Vincent* and Mr. Perry's *Hot Rod Pin-ups.* This book is Mr. Thomson's first for Motorbooks.

Alonso, Fernando "Ferny," 130–132
American Rodder, 98, 101
American Stamping, 123
Anderson, Dean, 35, 37, 38
Appleton, 44
Ardun, 83
Bakelite, 23
Bakersfield Blues, 81
Baron-Tatterfield, 104
Beatnik, The, 104
Beautiful Loser, 22
Big Sandy, 129
Binggeli, Ed, 89, 91
Bishop, Mike, 89
Black Sabbath, 43
Blasters, The, 129
Blink 182, 21
Blue bobber, 21, 22
Blue Collar Customs, 26–39
BMW, 13
"Border Lord," 143, 144
Bormann, Paul, 135
Boschetto, Paul, 85, 88
BRC, 99
Bridgeport, 81
Brizio, Roy, 120
Brodack, Bill, 51
Brookville, 82, 87, 131
Brookwood, 30
Buick, 31, 33, 67
Burley, Butch, 16
Butthole Surfers, 43
Cadillac, 30, 69, 75, 113, 136, 149, 153–155
California Hot Rods, 110–125
Camara, Gary, 89
Camaro, 37
Cannon, Phil, 28, 30, 33–35
Cannon, Rob, 28, 33–35
Car Craft, 31
Chapouris, Pete, 70, 120
Chavers, Sid, 72
Chevrolet, 20, 32, 37, 38, 49, 50, 55, 62, 68, 99, 104, 107, 114, 116, 117, 143, 144
Circle City Hot Rods, 126–139
Cobra, 88
Cochrane, Ryan, 82, 84, 87
Cockrell, Billy, 65, 67
Coddington, Boyd, 120, 130
Coonan, Steve, 153
Cooper, Stacy, 37
Cragar, 47
Craig's Interior Design, 155
Crown Customs, 35
Cruz, Jesse, 19, 23
Currie, 114
Custom Chrome, 23
Dalpoggetto, Ed, 87, 89
Damned, The, 43
De Soto, 104
Devil Deuce, The, 53

Dickerson, Wayne, 117
Dodge, 30
Doll Hut, The, 129
Duesenberg, 64
Edelbrock, 149
Edmunds, 131
El Camino, 43, 47, 62, 71, 72
Evans, Dale, 98
Fat Lucky's Upholstery, 61, 71–73, 75
Faust, Larry "Jungle," 81
Fear, 43
Fegley, Gary, 73
Firestone, 90
Ford, 14, 29, 30–33, 35, 37, 38, 47, 49, 51, 53, 73, 82–85, 86, 88, 90, 91, 97, 98, 101, 102, 114–117, 123, 124, 146–149
Fordor, 47, 118, 119, 123, 124
Foster, Cole, 10–25, 37, 120, 138
Foster, Pat, 13
Foster, Susan, 16, 17
Franco, Von, 115
Fretwell, Don, 16
Frye, Ron, 86
Fuller, Kent, 89
Gabe's Upholstery, 51
Gee, Chris, 61
General Motors, 67
Gibbon, Billy F, 7
Go-Nuts, 43
Gravelle brothers, 16
Griffith, Terry, 89
Halibrand, 85, 104, 107
Hamilton, Ryan, 118, 124
Hammett, Kirk, 12, 14, 17, 23, 37
Hanson, Eric, 107
Harley-Davidson, 22, 34
Harry Bradley Award, 148, 149
Hawes, Mike, 82, 85
Hetfield, James, 30, 33, 37
Hoffman, Paul, 102, 104, 107
Holland, Bill, 99
Holly, Buddy, 69
Holman Moody, 83, 85
Hop Up, 107
Hotrod Works, 104
Howard, Gary, 64–67, 74, 136, 140–157
Howard, Jo Ann, 150
Hutton, Charlie, 131
Impala, 32, 116, 145
Imperial, 30
Iron Horse, The, 51
Jackson, Kong, 65
Jacobs, Jim, 120
Jahn pistons, 123
Jard, Jim, 51, 53
Joehnck, Bob, 104
Johnstun, Sean, 61, 62, 70, 72–75
Jonckheere, Henri, 19
Joyoprayitno, Joh, 61
Kennedy, Jason and Joe, 40–57, 138

Kennedy, Joe Sr., 53
KH wires, 53
Kiwi Connection, 102, 104, 131, 132
Knapp, Carol, 53, 55, 102
Kovarik, Craig, 35
Kristofferson, Kris, 144
Leonardo, Tommy Jr., 102, 107
Lincoln, 35, 66, 82, 85, 88
Logsdon, John, 118, 121, 123, 124
Lonestar Round Up, 48
Mackenzie, Larry, 81, 91
Magnum, 114
Mandujano, Dave, 61, 70
McCulloch, 53
McKeane, Vernon, 66, 72, 75, 145, 151
Mercedes-Benz, 37, 38
"Mercury Blues," 64
Mercury, 69, 71, 98, 101, 104, 116, 123, 144, 150, 153
Metallica, 17, 37
MG, 37, 38
Millen, Rod, 130
Moore, Cory, 61
Morton, Mark, 107
Mugford, Hannah, 35
Mugford, Scott, 26–39
Muncie, 114, 135
Munson, Wade, 61
Mustang, 129
Nadine, 61, 64–68
Nancy, Tony, 72
Nomad, 30
Offenhauser, 49
Oldsmobile, 104, 130–132
Orbits, 29
Paladins, The, 129
Paso Robles, 23
Patterson, Andrew, 131
Pete & Jake's, 115
Peters, David, 81
Peterson, Dan, 61
Phaeton, 53
Phillips 66, 62
Powell, Rod, 145, 149
Pratt, Lee, 149, 155
Quinton, Jack, 104, 107
Ramirez, Mike, 61, 62
Rex Rod & Chassis, 78–93
Richards, Dan, 150, 153
Riviera, 71, 73, 148, 150
Roach's, 5
Rod & Custom, 53, 148
Rodder's Journal, The, 74, 153
Rodriguez, Mia, 100, 101, 104, 107
Rodriguez, Rudy, 94–109, 129, 138
Rodriguez, Sonny and Jasper, 97, 99–102, 104, 107
Rolls-Royce, 19

Ross Bava, 117
Runnels, Mercury Charlie, 58–77
Sadletzky, Eric, 90
Sales, Jesus, 135
Salinas Boys Customs, 10–25
San Francisco Rod and Custom Show, 85
Scott, Russell, 129
Serrano, Eddie, 90
Sexton, Charlie, 64
Sharp heads, 90, 104
Shifters, The, 129
Shimer, Dan, 118
Shine, Jimmy, 51, 120, 129
Skow, Jordan, 16, 19, 23
Sledge, Kevin "Sinus," 129
Smith, Dave, 13
Smith, Kristi, 113, 118, 123
Smith, Leroy, 113, 116, 118, 123, 124
Smith, Mike, 110–125, 138
Smith, Mitch and Robby, 113, 118, 123
SO-CAL Speed Shop, 44
Soliday, Lance, 44, 47, 48, 51, 55
South Austin Speed Shop, 58–77
Speed Week, 37
Stairs, Brian, 99
Steve's Restorations, 90
Stevens, Job, 16, 23
Stromberg, 90, 131
Studebaker, 29, 30, 68
Tardel, Keith, 78–93
Tardel, Mary, 85
Tardel, Vern, 86, 87, 89, 91, 118, 120, 123
Thickstun intake, 90
Thomas, George and Buck, 16
Topolino, 113, 117, 118, 123, 124
Torjeson, Thomas, 16, 19, 23
Toyota, 31, 33
Trinidad, Drew, 31, 33
Tudor, 37
Two-Lane Blacktop, 62
Vaughan, Jimmie, 144, 146, 148–152, 154
Violet Vision, 148
Volkswagen, 115
Wertheimer, Steve, 149
Westergard Motors, 19
White, Jimmy, 120, 126–139
White, Michelle, 136, 138
Wiegel, Todd, 117
Willits, Craig, 155
Wilwood disc system, 33
Winfield cam, 123
Wurlitzer, 69
Young, Mike, 145, 149, 153
Youngblood, Kenny, 13
Youth Brigade, 43